The country side of cooking

Recipes compiled by Caroline Ellwood

Published for Ovaltine by
Spectator Publications Limited

Produced and published by
Spectator Publications Limited
©1974
Printing by Tinling (1973) Limited   SBN 900869 22 4

Contents

The reproductions within this book are of wood engravings by Thomas Bewick (1753-1828) and some of his notable contemporaries.

Introduction

The best dishes in British cookery are probably those that originated in farmhouses where cooking was a simple art, yet still one that abounded in skills as subtle as the flavours given to the dishes by herbs and fresh produce from the region. Whilst other countries may excel in presenting their food when it has been enhanced by rich sauces and highly flavoured spices, the cooks of this country have become renowned for serving wholesome food cooked so well that nourishment and goodness is retained but the meals still appeal to the family in taste and appearance. Meat puddings, steaming roly-polys, pans of thick soup and rich, creamy rice puddings will not be considered dull fare if they have once been tasted when prepared in traditional ways.

However, country cooking is distinguished not only by simplicity but also by the almost exclusive use of fresh produce. We have all become so accustomed to tinned and packaged food that we tend to forget how many products – such as bread, soups, pickles, jam, sausages and custard – were originally made from fresh ingredients, and were altogether a different thing from the mass-produced food we eat so easily and so often nowadays. It is probably a rebellion against the bland taste of so much food today that causes housewives in the towns to hanker after the fresh goods so easily available to country cooks; and the quick sale of fresh brown eggs, free-range poultry and home-grown vegetables proves that even a slight increase in cost is not a deterrent to anyone who wants to feed a

family with the best food available. Mrs. Beeton's misquoted and much-ridiculed injunction to 'take two dozen fresh eggs' for so many of her dishes is perhaps an exaggeration, but certainly there is a tendency now to add more fresh produce than ever before. Because we have become so accustomed to cooking ingredients that are sometimes rather tasteless inevitably our style has become adapted to such food, and many recipes in use today are not really suitable for preparing fresh food since the delicate flavour of some things, especially fish, fruit and vegetables, can be lost through heavy-handed cooking.

For this reason Ovaltine, who have for many years been associated with everything that is nutritious and wholesome in country goodness, have chosen the recipes

for this book in the hope that they will help many people to discover the delicious taste of country cooking, and also to see how easily you can prepare for yourself a a number of foods that have reached your table before only in packaged forms. Years ago when travel was difficult it was often impossible for many cooks to find out more about food preparation than they could learn from other women in their village. Without any forms of mass communication the local cooking traditions became tightly confined to small areas; and it is recipes for regional cooking of this kind that Ovaltine have included in their book. Many recipes have been gleaned from old records passed down from one housewife to another, each one tracing its origins back to old farm kitchens, grand manor houses or tiny, long-forgotten hamlets.

The variety of processes and the vast quantities of food that a country housewife encountered every day meant that she needed good equipment in her kitchen. Compared with most cooks today she had very few items, but everything was designed for a purpose and constantly in use. Gleaming copper saucepans in many sizes hung on the wall, knives were sharp, mincing bowls could be used to reduce anything to tiny shreds and a mortar and pestle was ideal for grinding up herbs and spices. It is no coincidence that a revival of interest in country cooking should have come at a time when more and more manufacturers are producing kitchen equipment of all kinds that compares favourably with the utensils in an old-fashioned farmhouse. Solid well-made saucepans, sturdy wooden spoons, stone jars, wood and earthenware used instead of plastic: suddenly old designs are popular again, and in spite of modern innovations many gadgets owe much to the well-tried efficiency of old methods, even to the imitation of spit-roasting that is incorporated into the most up-to-date cookers. Crockery designs echo farmhouse china, much of the oven-to-tableware closely resembles old-style casseroles and treasures from antique shops, such as chestnut roasters and long-handled toasting forks, are valued for their excellent qualities, both practical and decorative.

It is unlikely that many people will be able to prepare their food on a white deal table in a stone-flagged kitchen where home-cured hams hang from darkened beams and a kettle sings over an open fire; but this does not mean that housewives should neglect the recipes we have inherited from such kitchens. It is the aim of this book to show that excellent fresh food can be prepared by anyone, whether they have their own produce to use or whether they get supplies from the shops. Convenience foods are excellent for emergencies, but they should not be used every day when it is easy to acquire the country habit of cooking which is so much better for your family.

Herbs

Herbs and spices have always played an important part in the lives of country people, not only as flavourings for cookery but also as the basis for medicines, charms and cosmetics. Farmer's wives were surrounded by wild plants to provide flavourings for food or cures for minor ailments. They experimented with the plants they found in the hedgerows, discovered the different tastes, and properties, and used them appropriately, whether for perfuming the linen cupboard or soothing an illness.

By trial and error sprigs of plants were added to hot and cold dishes to see if they enhanced the dish or detracted from it. Perhaps the herbs were better used whole and removed before serving; or crushed, or added at the end of cooking, or used only as a garnish. Plants with a pungent flavour and aroma, such as sage, thyme and members of the onion family were soon widely used. As the cooks searched for these familiar herbs they came across other more unusual ones and they too were included in recipes; and the secrets and properties which each plant contained were handed down from generation to generation.

For convenience the most popular kinds of plants were moved to a corner of the kitchen garden, and with extra care and cultivation the plants flourished and multiplied. Whilst country gardens used to grow borage, marjoram, tarragon and pennyroyal together with many other less familiar herbs, the modern household has

sadly reduced its herb garden to a root of parsley and perhaps one kind of mint. With a renewal of interest in the taste and use of fresh herbs more cooks are being tempted to grow their own plants. Cultivation is easy, even for the inexperienced gardener because many firms now offer a wide assortment of small well-established plants that can be grown successfully in window boxes or tubs even if space is limited; or you can reserve a special corner of the garden for herb growing. Most varieties can be raised from seed, with a little care, and planted out in window boxes or the garden. So, fresh herbs are within everyones' reach.

For culinary purposes it is much better to use fresh herbs, but obviously there are times of the year when they are not available. Herbs are easily preserved by picking on a sunny day and drying them as quickly as possible so that they do not lose too much flavour. Herbs with small leaves, such as savory and thyme, can be dried by tying in small bundles and hanging in a warm kitchen or airing cupboard. The larger leaves of herbs such as mint, bay and sage, should be stripped from the stalks, laid on a wire rack and placed in a warm, dry atmosphere.

When the leaves are dry and brittle they can be lightly crushed and stored in air-tight jars or tins in a cool, dark place. If you are unable to preserve your own herbs, buy small quantities of commercially dried ones from a reputable shop with a high turnover of stock, to ensure that the herbs are not stale.

Herb vinegars are expensive to buy, but they can easily be made at home and are delicious when used in cooking or in salad dressings. Fill a clean empty vinegar bottle a quarter full with freshly picked herbs – tarragon is excellent – and fill the rest with hot wine vinegar. Cork the bottle, and leave for a month. The vinegar may then be decanted and used when required.

Huge bushes of lavender grew in the country gardens, and the dried flowers were tied in muslin bags – often decorated with elaborate ribbons and embroidery – and used to keep linen and clothes fresh and free from moths. Fresh lavender water was sprinkled over the sheets as they were ironed to give a sweet smell while they were being used. Pot pourri, a mixture of dried flowers, leaves and spices, was often kept in special jars which were opened each evening to perfume the room. Satin pillows filled with hops or a mixture of herbs were used to induce sleep and perhaps sweet dreams as well. But now, when all kinds of cosmetics are produced from manufactured chemicals it is hard to imagine that not so long ago the country housewives relied on homemade distillations of such herbs as witchhazel, rosewater, elderflowers and lime blossom to preserve their complexions.

Country people also depended very largely on homemade preparations such as camomile or lime bud tea, and other *tisanes* to cure headaches, indigestion, fever and many other common ailments. It was difficult for a doctor to call regularly and the farming communities preferred to be self-sufficient, treating themselves and their animals for mild complaints. Even today some people prefer these old remedies to drugs, and they can be surprisingly effective. The countryside still has much to offer us and we, like the country communities of yesterday, should make the most of it.

Herb	Description	Uses
Basil	A sweet aromatic leaf from two kinds of plant, bush basil which is a small short-stemmed plant and sweet basil which is a taller plant with longer pointed leaves	Soups Sauces Fish dishes or with Tomatoes
Bay	The bay tree belongs to the laurel family. The flavour is mild, sweet and musky	Soups Stews Casseroles Milk puddings
Borage	A tall plant with blue flowers. Both the leaves and flowers are used and have a faint cucumber flavour	Fruit Wine cups Salads
Chervil	A type of parsley which has a delicate sweet taste and fragrant aroma	Sauces Salads Omelettes
Chives	A member of the onion family. It is a bulb with fine grass-like leaves and has a purple flower. The leaves have a delicate onion flavour	Salads Sauces Omelettes
Dill	A feathery-leaved plant which has a mild aroma and a slightly sweet caraway flavour	Pickles Fish Salads Apple pie
Fennel	A tall perennial with feathery leaves and a sweet aniseed flavour with a slight taste of celery	Fish Pork Salads
Garlic	A bulb related to the onion family. Each bulb is made of cloves. It has a pungent and lingering flavour and aroma	Soup Stews Salads Sauces Savoury dishes

Horseradish	A perennial with long leaves. The root is the part used and this has a pungent hot and biting taste	Sauces Meat Trout Stuffings
Lemon Thyme	An aromatic plant with a lemon flavour	Fish Pork Custards Jellies Salads
Marigold	The part used is the petal of the flower. It has a rich but subtle flavour	Soups Stews Salads
Marjoram	There are two types, the sweet marjoram, which is an annual, and the pot marjoram, which is a perennial. Both have an aromatic savoury flavour	Soups Sauces Stuffings Salads
Mint	There are about fourteen varieties (e.g. spearmint, curly, apple mint, pennyroyal). It has a pungent flavour	Sauce Potatoes Peas Lamb Preserves
Parsley	A biennial herb with deep green curly leaves	Garnish Sauces Stuffings Egg dishes
Rosemary	A small shrub with narrow greyish-green leaves and a pungent aromatic sweet flavour	Lamb Soups Stews Veal
Sage	A shrub-like perennial with grey-green leaves. It has a bold, slightly bitter taste	Stuffings Fish Minced meat
Savory	There are two types, an annual summer savory and a perennial winter type. Both varieties have narrow leaves and a pungent spicy flavour	Omelettes Soups Salads Stuffings Cooked cheese dishes
Sorrel	A wild herb with a strongly acid flavour	Cook with Spinach Salads Soups
Tarragon	A perennial herb with narrow deep green leaves. There are two types, French and Russian. It has a strong aromatic flavour reminiscent of aniseed	Sauces Egg dishes Salads Fish
Thyme	A herb with small shiny leaves, and a strong pungent and aromatic flavour resembling clove	Chicken Stuffings Soups Hare

Spice	Description	Uses
Allspice	This is the dried fruit of the allspice or pimento tree. Darkish red in colour, rather like peppercorns. The flavour resembles a mixture of clove, cinnamon and nutmeg	Potted meat Pickling Cakes Pies Relishes Preserves
Aniseed	The dried ripe fruit of the anise plant. The seeds are a greenish-grey colour and contain a volatile oil with a warm sweet aromatic taste and odour	Puddings Pancakes Breads Buns Cheese dishes
Caraway Seeds	The small, brown hard seeds of a feathery plant. The leaves are sometimes used. It has a pronounced and pervasive flavour	Seed cakes Rye bread Cheese Soups Meats
Cardamom Seed	The fruit of perennial cardamom, which is a member of the ginger family. Available with or without the pod, and whole or ground. There is a suggestion of eucalyptus in the flavour	Cakes Gingerbread Sausages Pickles Apple pies
Cayenne	Prepared from small bright red and very pungent chillies which are pounded down to a powder	Curries Smoked fish Cooked cheese

Cinnamon	The bark of a species of laurel, the paper thin bark being rolled as a stick cinnamon or powdered. It is a pungent, sweet spice	Cakes Biscuits Buns Preserves
Clove	The dried unopened buds of the myrtle, similar in shape to small nails and reddish brown in colour. Cloves are very aromatic, warming and yet astringent in their action	Apple Preserves Bread sauce Bacon
Coriander Seed	A small round dried fruit which is yellowish brown in colour. The flavour is aromatic and very fresh, with a suggestion of orange	Duck Game Junkets Custards Cakes Biscuits
Cumin	The fruit is similar in appearance to caraway seeds, but the flavour is harsher and has bitter undertones	Pork Cheese dishes Curry powder
Ginger	The dried root of a tropical plant. The root is used whole or ground and has an aromatic hot, biting and pungent flavour	Cakes Gingerbread Puddings Pickling
Mace	The dried fibrous network which grows round the nutmeg seed is a golden colour and has a flavour like nutmeg, but milder and less sweet. It is used ground or in blade form	Used whole in sauces soups Used powdered in cakes Fish sauces
Nutmeg	The pit, or seed, of the nutmeg fruit. Available ground and whole (for grating as required). Nutmeg has a sweet, warm and aromatic flavour	Puddings Sauces Mashed potatoes
Paprika	A bright red powder obtained from a sweeter type of chilli than cayenne. There are two varieties, either with a sweet mild flavour, or with a slight bite	A spice used as a garnish to give an appetising appearance to meat, fish, egg and cheese dishes

Peppercorns	The dried unopened fruit of a climbing vine-like plant which grows wild. The black peppercorns are the unripe green peppercorns which are dried in the sun until the surface becomes black and wrinkled. White pepper comes from the ripe red peppercorns after the protective pericarp has been rubbed off. Pepper brings out the flavour of savoury food, the black type having a stronger and more pungent taste than white	Soups Sauces Meat Fish Stuffings Pickles
Poppy Seeds	Tiny, greyish-black seeds from the poppy plant, with a distinctive mild and nutty flavour	As a garnish on rolls and bread
Saffron	The dried stamen of the saffron crocus. The best saffron to buy is in the form of whole styles which should be infused in hot water before using. It gives a bright yellow appearance to food and imparts a mild fragrant flavour	Buns Cakes Rice
Turmeric	A perennial plant of the ginger family. The dried root is a yellow orange colour and has an aromatic warm and musky flavour	Curry powder Piccalilli
Vanilla	The dried pods of a tropical orchid. The pods are dark brown, long and plump with a slightly oily look. It is the sweetest of all spices	Custards Ices Cakes

The problem facing a country housewife is how to cope with a hungry family, all with hearty appetites, who come in from working on the land and need hot, nourishing food. There will probably be farm workers, visitors or friends calling too, so the obvious answer is a large pot of soup. However, whilst the recipes evolved in the country make the most of readily available and economical ingredients they are not only for the farming family – every household will benefit from home-made soup.

The basis of many soups is stock, made by simmering a chicken carcase and giblets, beef or veal bones, or the remains of a leg of lamb. Most of the recipes in this section depend on good stock, so fewer additional ingredients are needed – which cuts down on cost as well as on preparation time – to create entirely original flavours. If possible, use freshly gathered produce from your own garden or buy the vegetables from a reputable greengrocer – since fresh vegetables give a good flavour and lots of nutrients. Lentils and split peas are included in several recipes to thicken and enrich the soups and although they are available in most shops they are often overlooked as possible ingredients for interesting dishes. In the recipe for Cottage Pea Soup some of the pods, which are usually thrown away, are included in the broth which gives it an unusually good flavour. Oxtail soup, which makes use of an economical cut of meat, provides a meal in itself, if served with hot bread and cheese, and followed by fresh fruit, and will satisfy even the heartiest appetite. Cullen Skink, a local name for a fish soup, makes a tasty, and different, start to a meal.

Cock-a-Leekie, Mulligatawny and Scotch Broth are commonplace soups on our tables, but sadly we settle too often for the canned and packaged varieties. Although these make very acceptable substitutes in an emergency, the recipes in this section will show that homemade soups are neither difficult to make nor take a long time to prepare. Probably because instant soups are so easily available we have forgotten how much visitors appreciate a cook's effort in producing homemade soup; and once you have basked in the glow of achievement by presenting your own broth or soup you will be unlikely to serve anything else again.

Cream of Celery Soup

Serves 4 – 6

1 ounce butter
1 large onion, sliced into rings
1 large head of celery, scrubbed and sliced
1 pint milk
1 pint chicken stock
A bunch of herbs
3 tablespoons plain flour
¼ pint milk
3 tablespoons double cream
Chives, chopped

Melt the butter in a large pan and fry the onion gently for 5 minutes. Add the celery and continue frying until the vegetables are soft.

Pour in the milk and stock, add the bunch of herbs then bring to the boil and simmer for 1 hour, or until the vegetables are thoroughly cooked. Remove the herbs and pour the soup through a sieve or blend it in a liquidiser.

Return the liquid to the pan, blend the flour and a quarter of a pint of milk together and stir this into the soup. Bring it to the boil and simmer for 5 minutes, stirring occasionally.

Adjust the seasoning to taste, and stir in the cream and chopped chives just before serving.

Cock-A-Leekie

Serves 4

1 x 3 pound boiling chicken
2 pints stock or water
6 medium sized leeks, washed and sliced
    into 1 inch rings
A bunch of herbs
1 teaspoon lemon juice
½ pound prunes, soaked overnight
Parsley, chopped

Remove the giblets from the chicken and wash these with the bird, draining well. Place in a large pan and cover with the stock.

Add the leeks, herbs and lemon juice to the pan and season well with salt and pepper. Bring to the boil and simmer for 3 hours, or until the meat is very tender. Add the drained prunes and cook for a further ½ hour. Cut the meat off the carcase of the chicken and remove the giblets and the bunch of herbs from the pan.

Serve the soup with the pieces of chicken in it; or use just half the meat, and keep the rest for a pie or some other dish that requires cooked chicken meat.

Serve this soup very hot, with parsley sprinkled into it at the last moment.

Mulligatawny

Serves 4 – 6

2 ounces dripping
2 large onions, chopped
2 ounces plain flour
½ ounce curry powder
1 tablespoon tomato purée
2 pints beef stock
4 ounces patna rice

Melt the dripping in a pan and fry the onions until they are golden brown. Mix in the flour and curry powder and cook for 5 minutes, stirring well.

Add the tomato purée and beef stock and season with salt and pepper. Bring to the boil and simmer for ½ hour. Cook the rice in boiling, salted water for 12 – 15 minutes or until it is just cooked, and then drain it.

Just before serving stir the rice into the soup, adjust the seasoning, bring to the boil and simmer for 4 – 5 minutes.

Thick and Nourishing Oxtail Soup

Serves 6

1 large oxtail
1 ounce seasoned flour
1 ounce dripping
1 large onion, chopped
1 turnip, chopped
1 stick of celery, chopped
4 pints water
A bunch of herbs
2 ounces butter
2 ounces plain flour
1 tablespoon lemon juice
¼ pint sherry or claret

Cut the oxtail into pieces, trimming away any excess fat. Wash and dry the meat, then toss each piece in seasoned flour. Melt the dripping in a large pan and fry the oxtail gently until it is browned all over.

Add the vegetables to the pan with the water and bunch of herbs. Season well with salt and pepper and simmer gently for 3 hours.

Allow to cool slightly and strain the soup. Remove all the meat from the bones and keep this on one side.

Melt the butter in a pan, stir in the flour and cook for 5 minutes, allowing the mixture to brown slightly. Take care it does not burn because this will ruin the flavour of the soup.

Gradually mix in the liquid, and bring it to the boil stirring all the time. Add the meat, the lemon juice and sherry or claret and cook for a further 5 minutes.

Cottage Pea Soup

Serves 4

1 pound green peas
½ ounce butter
1 small onion, sliced into rings
A sprig of mint
A sprig of parsley
1 pint white stock
2 teaspoons flour
4 tablespoons milk
1 tablespoon double cream

Shell the peas, rinse them in cold water, and wash one third of the pods. Melt the butter in the pan and cook the onion until it is transparent. Stir the peas into the butter and onion mixture.

Add the pea pods, mint, parsley, stock, salt and pepper and simmer for 1 hour. Using a wooden spoon, rub the soup through a wire sieve or blend it in a liquidiser. Return the liquid to the pan and thicken with the blended flour and milk. Bring to the boil, stirring continually, then adjust the seasoning to taste. Finally stir in the cream and serve at once.

Lentil Pottage

Serves 4 – 6

½ pound lentils
2 large onions, sliced into rings
2 carrots, chopped
2 sticks of celery, chopped
1½ pints stock or water
2 sprigs of thyme
2 sprigs of parsley
½ ounce butter

Wash the lentils and soak overnight in a covered bowl. Drain off the water and place them in a large saucepan with the sliced onions, carrots and celery.

Pour the stock over the vegetables and add the herbs, salt and pepper. Bring the soup to the boil and simmer for 1½ hours. Pass the mixture through a sieve, or blend in in a liquidiser and return the liquid to the pan. If the soup is too thick, add some hot stock to adjust the consistency.

Before serving, stir in the butter and serve very hot.

Scotch Broth

Serves 6

1 pound scrag end of lamb
4 ounces pearl barley
3 pints stock or water
1 large carrot, diced
1 turnip, diced
2 large onions, diced
1 stick of celery, diced
1 tablespoon parsley, chopped

Trim the meat and cut into pieces. Wash the barley and put it with the bones and meat into a large saucepan, pour in the stock and season with salt and pepper. Bring to the boil and skim carefully.

Simmer the broth for 2 hours. Remove the bones and add the carrot, turnip and onions simmering for a further ¾ hour or until the vegetables are cooked. Just before serving, sprinkle with the chopped parsley.

Cream of Carrot Soup

Serves 4 – 6

1 ounce butter
1 pound carrots, chopped
1 stick celery, chopped
1 small turnip, chopped
1 small onion, chopped
1 ounce bacon, chopped
1½ pints of white stock
A bunch of herbs
3 level tablespoons flour
¼ pint milk
2 tablespoons cream
Parsley, chopped

Melt the butter in a saucepan and fry the vegetables for 5 minutes. Add the bacon and cook for a further 3 minutes. Gradually stir in the stock, and add the herbs. Season well with salt and pepper.

Bring the soup to the boil, and simmer for 1 hour, until the vegetables are soft.

Remove the herbs, and pass the soup through a wire sieve, or blend it in a liquidiser. Return the soup to the pan. Blend the flour and milk together and stir this into the pan. Bring to the boil and cook for 3 minutes. Adjust the seasoning and add the cream. Sprinkle the parsley over the top and serve at once.

Country Potato Soup

Serves 6

2 pounds potatoes peeled and
   cut into large squares
3 large onions, chopped
2 ounces butter
Stock
1½ pints milk
¼ pint cream
1 tablespoon chives, chopped

Place the potatoes and onions in a large
pan with the butter, and cook gently for 10
minutes without letting the contents turn
brown.

Add sufficient stock to cover the vegetables, season with salt and pepper and cook
for ¾ hour, or until the potatoes and onions
are soft. Rub the mixture through a sieve,
or blend it in a liquidiser and return the
soup to the pan.

Stir in the milk and bring the liquid to
the boil, stirring continually, then remove
the pan from the heat and add the cream.
Sprinkle the top of the soup with chopped
chives and serve at once.

Watercress Soup

Serves 6

2 ounces butter
1 large onion, chopped
½ pound potatoes, peeled and chopped
½ pint stock
1½ pints milk
2 bunches of watercress, cleaned
A pinch of ground nutmeg
2 teaspoons cornflour
1 tablespoon milk
2 tablespoons double cream

Melt the butter in a pan and cook the
onion until it is soft but not brown. Add the
potatoes and stock, bring to the boil and
cook gently for 15 minutes. Stir in the milk
and simmer for a further 10 minutes.

Add the watercress to the pan, reserving
a little for garnish. Cook for 10 minutes
and then sieve the mixture or blend it in a
liquidiser. Return the soup to the pan,
season to taste with salt, pepper and nutmeg. Blend the cornflour and 1 tablespoon
milk together and stir this into the soup.

Bring to the boil and cook for 1 minute.
Remove from the heat and stir in the cream.
Serve at once.

Cullen Skink

Serves 4

2 pounds smoked haddock, skinned
1 onion, sliced into rings
$1\frac{1}{2}$ pints milk
About $\frac{1}{2}$ pound cooked potatoes, mashed
2 ounces butter, cut into small pieces

Poach the haddock in a little water for about 5 minutes. Add the sliced onion and continue cooking for a further 10 minutes. Take the haddock out, and remove all the flesh from the bones. Flake this roughly and return it to the pan, seasoning with freshly ground pepper. Simmer for about 20 minutes and then strain off the fish stock.

Put the milk and stock in a pan together with the fish and bring it to the boil. Add mashed potato until the soup has thickened to a creamy consistency, then season to taste. Stir in the butter and serve at once.

Farmhouse Onion Soup

Serves 6

6 large onions, chopped
2 ounces butter
2 pints milk
2 tablespoons flour
2 tablespoons milk

Cook the onions gently in the butter until they are soft but not brown. Add the milk, season with salt and pepper, blend the flour and 2 tablespoons milk together and stir this into the milk and onion mixture.

Bring the soup to the boil, stirring all the time, and simmer for 5 minutes. Adjust the seasoning and serve very hot.

Ham and Pea Hotchpotch

Serves 6

$\frac{1}{2}$ pound split peas
3 pints boiling water
1 ham bone
1 large onion, finely chopped
A bunch of herbs
1 bayleaf

Soak the peas overnight in cold water. After draining, place them in a large pan, pour in the boiling water, add the ham bone, onion, herbs and season with salt and pepper.

Bring to the boil, simmer for 2 hours or until the peas are tender. Before serving, remove the ham bone, bunch of herbs and bayleaf.

A Simple Leek Soup

Serves 4

2 ounces beef dripping
4 leeks, washed and chopped
1 pound potatoes, peeled and diced
2 pints chicken stock or water
2 tablespoons cream

Melt the dripping in a pan and fry the leeks gently until they are a light golden colour.

Add the potatoes and fry for 5 – 10 minutes. Pour in the stock, bring to the boil, season well with salt and pepper and simmer for 2 hours.

Adjust the seasoning to taste, remove from the heat and add the cream. Serve at once.

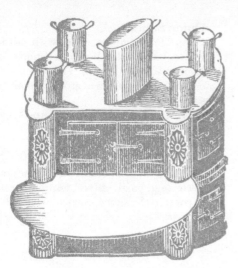

Cracklements, Sauces and Stuffings

Whilst most of the recipes in this book emphasise the simplicity of cooking wholesome food in the most natural way, many foods are enhanced by the imaginative addition of a sauce, relish or stuffing.

From necessity many people have become accustomed to bottled mint sauce, horse-radish relish, canned apple sauce and cranberry jelly in jars, and it will come as a surprise to discover how different – and how special – the same thing becomes when it is made at home. Stewed apples, sieved and sweetened with a little brown sugar, can make a sauce as tempting as the pork with which it is served. Once you have encountered the delicate flavour of fresh mint sauce you will not easily be persuaded to return to the strongly flavoured com-mercial preparations. Mint sauce keeps well too, so make use of the summer abundance of mint and store enough to accompany roast lamb during the winter months.

Although sauces may be considered as an 'extra' to the meat or main dish, it must be remembered that they not only com-plement the food, but also add flavour and goodness to the family meal. A basic sauce mixture can be flavoured with any of the ingredients listed in the recipes, but you can vary and experiment with anything you choose. It is not necessary to be lavish with the flavours you add, as you will dis-cover when you see how little fresh chopped parsley is needed to transform the taste of a plain white sauce.

The section of recipes on traditional country stuffings will introduce many cooks to new flavour combinations: try Lamb served with Apricot Stuffing, Ham filled with Savoury Stuffing, homemade Sage and Onion Stuffing for pork and Sausage Forcemeat or Chestnut Stuffing for poultry.

The majority of sauces are for use with the main course of a meal, but there are recipes for several sweet ones as well: Brandy Butter, the traditional companion for Christmas Pudding, and Butterscotch Sauce which when poured over ice cream will gain new popularity with the children.

Basic White Sauce Recipes

Coating Sauce
1 ounce butter
1 ounce flour
½ pint milk or stock

Pouring Sauce
¾ ounce butter
¾ ounce flour
½ pint milk or stock

Melt the butter in a pan, stir in the flour and cook for 2 minutes. Gradually stir in the liquid, bring to the boil and cook for 3 minutes. Season to taste and use the mixture as a basis for many savoury sauces.

Some examples are given below:

Egg Sauce
Chop a hard boiled egg and add it to the basic recipe, together with a teaspoon of chopped chives. Season well with salt and pepper.

Parsley Sauce
Make the sauce in the usual way, season with salt and pepper and add 2 tablespoons chopped parsley and 1 teaspoon lemon juice.

Shrimp or Prawn Sauce
Add 2 ounces fresh or canned shrimps or prawns to the sauce. Season with salt and pepper, then stir in 1 teaspoon lemon juice and a few drops of anchovy essence.

Cheese Sauce
Add 2 – 3 ounces grated cheese to the sauce and 1 teaspoon mixed mustard. Season well with salt, pepper and cayenne pepper.

Mushroom Sauce
Chop 2 ounces mushrooms and cook gently in ½ ounce butter. Add to the basic sauce and season with salt and pepper.

Mustard Sauce
Blend together 1 tablespoon English mustard, 1 tablespoon vinegar and a little sugar and stir into the sauce.

Caper Sauce
Roughly chop 2 tablespoons capers and add these with 2 teaspoons vinegar to the basic sauce. Season with salt and pepper.

Onion Sauce
Chop 2 large onions, cover with salted water, bring to the boil and simmer for 12 minutes. Drain well. The onion water can be used in place of stock to make the sauce.

Stir in the chopped onions and season with salt and pepper.

Herb Sauce
Add 2 – 3 tablespoons of mixed chopped herbs (e.g. basil, chives, fennel, parsley, thyme) to the sauce. Season with salt and pepper.

Horseradish Sauce
2 tablespoons grated horseradish
1 teaspoon lemon juice
1 teaspoon vinegar
2 teaspoons caster sugar
A pinch of dry mustard
¼ pint double cream

Mix the horseradish, lemon juice, vinegar, sugar and mustard together. Whip the cream until it is fairly stiff, then stir in the horseradish mixture.

This is a traditional relish to serve with beef.

Mint Sauce

3 tablespoons mint, chopped finely
1 tablespoon caster sugar
2 tablespoons boiling water
2 tablespoons malt vinegar

Place the mint on a chopping board, add half the sugar and chop together.

Put the mint into a sauceboat, sprinkle the remaining sugar over it and pour in the boiling water. Mix well, allow to cool then add the vinegar.

Serve with lamb.

Cranberry Sauce

½ pound fresh cranberries
½ pound sugar
½ pint water
2 tablespoons port or red wine

Wash the cranberries and drain well. Dissolve the sugar in the water and boil for 5 minutes.

Add the cranberries, return to the boil and cook for 10 minutes, or until the fruit is soft.

Stir in the port and serve with turkey or chicken.

Apple Sauce

1 pound Bramley cooking apples, peeled, cored and sliced
A pinch of ground cloves
A pinch of ground nutmeg
2 tablespoons water
1 ounce butter
Sugar

Place the apples in a pan, add the spices and water and simmer gently until the fruit is soft.

Beat in the butter, add sugar to taste, and serve with pork and sausages.

Gooseberry Sauce

½ pound gooseberries
2 tablespoons water
A pinch of mixed spice
1 ounce butter
1 – 2 ounces sugar

Top and tail the gooseberries, wash and place them in a pan with the water.

Simmer for about 10 minutes, or until the fruit is soft.

Stir in the mixed spice and butter, and sweeten to taste with the sugar.

Serve with mackerel.

Butterscotch Sauce

2 ounces butter
2 ounces soft brown sugar
1 level tablespoon golden syrup
Juice and grated rind of a lemon
1 ounce walnuts, chopped

Melt the butter in a pan, stir in the sugar and syrup. Boil for 2 minutes, or until the mixture is just thickening and turning to caramel.

Remove from the heat, stir in the lemon rind and juice and chopped walnuts.

Serve over ice cream or with steamed puddings.

Egg Custard Sauce

2 small eggs
1 level tablespoon sugar
½ pint milk
A few drops of vanilla essence

Whisk the eggs and sugar lightly. Warm the milk in a heavy based pan, add the vanilla essence and leave to stand for 10 minutes.

Pour the warm milk over the eggs whisking all the time.

Stir over a gentle heat until the sauce thickens and can glaze the back of a spoon.

Serve hot or cold with fruit or sponge puddings.

Brandy Butter

¼ pound butter
¼ pound soft brown sugar
3 – 4 tablespoons brandy
A few drops of lemon juice

Cream the butter until it is light and fluffy.
Beat in the sugar gradually, adding a little
brandy and lemon juice at a time taking
care that the mixture does not curdle.

Beat the sauce until it is pale and frothy.
Pile into a small serving dish and leave to
harden before serving.

Serve with Christmas pudding or mince
pies.

Tomato Sauce

1 ounce butter or oil
1 small onion, chopped
1 small carrot, chopped
1 ounce bacon, chopped
1 medium-sized can tomatoes
¼ pint chicken stock
A bunch of herbs
1 bayleaf
A pinch of sugar
1 teaspoon lemon juice
½ ounce cornflour
2 tablespoons stock or water

Melt the butter in a pan and gently fry the
onion and carrot together for 5 minutes,
add the chopped bacon and cook for a
further 5 minutes. Add the tomatoes, stock,
herbs, sugar, lemon juice and season well
with salt and pepper.

Bring to the boil and simmer for 30 – 45
minutes, or until the vegetables are
cooked.

Pass the sauce through a sieve and return
to the pan. Blend the cornflour with the
stock or water and add to the tomato sauce.
Bring to the boil, stirring continually and
simmer for 5 minutes.

Adjust the seasoning to taste and serve.

Cumberland Sauce

1 large orange
1 large lemon
4 tablespoons redcurrant jelly
4 tablespoons red wine
2 level teaspoons cornflour
2 tablespoons water

Peel the rind from the orange and lemon,
taking care not to include any of the white
pith. Cut it into very thin strips, place these
in a pan, cover with water and cook for 5
minutes until they are soft, then drain
them.

Extract the juice from the fruit, strain it
into a pan, add the redcurrant jelly stirring
until it dissolves then cook for 5 minutes
and add the wine. Blend the cornflour and
water together and add this to the sauce.
Bring to the boil, stirring until it thickens.

Return the strips of orange and lemon
rind to the sauce. Heat through and serve
with ham, venison, lamb and mutton.

Bread Sauce

4 cloves
1 medium-sized onion
1 blade of mace
1 bayleaf
3 peppercorns
½ pint milk
2 ounces fresh white breadcrumbs
½ ounce butter
2 tablespoons cream

Stick the cloves into the onion and place it
in a saucepan with the herbs, peppercorns
and milk.

Bring to the boil slowly then remove from
the heat and leave covered for 1 – 2 hours.

Remove the mace, bayleaf and peppercorns and add the breadcrumbs and butter.
Mix well and allow to cook very slowly for
about 15 minutes, then remove the onion.

Stir in the cream and serve with chicken
turkey or pheasant.

Chestnut Stuffing

1 pound fresh chestnuts
½ pint milk
1 ounce butter
1 onion, finely chopped
2 ounces bacon, chopped
¼ pound fresh white breadcrumbs
1 level teaspoon parsley, chopped
½ ounce butter, melted
Grated rind of a lemon
1 egg, beaten

Boil the chestnuts for 5 minutes to soften them, drain and remove the brown skins.

Simmer the peeled chestnuts in the milk for 40 minutes, or until they are soft. Drain well and pass them through a sieve or blend in a liquidiser.

Melt the butter in a pan and fry the onion gently until it is transparent, add the bacon and cook for a further 5 minutes. Remove the pan from the heat and stir in the breadcrumbs, parsley, melted butter, lemon rind and season well with salt and pepper.

Add the chestnut purée and mix well. Bind with the beaten egg.

The quantities given in this recipe produce enough stuffing for a 10 pound turkey; but the amounts can be varied according to the size of bird that you are cooking.

Sage and Onion Stuffing

4 large onions, chopped
½ pound fresh white breadcrumbs
1½ ounces butter, melted
6 sage leaves, chopped finely
1 egg, beaten

Cook the onions in boiling water for about 10 minutes, or until they are tender. Drain well.

Mix the breadcrumbs, melted butter and chopped sage leaves together and season with salt and pepper.

Add the chopped onion and mix well. If necessary stir in a little beaten egg to bind the mixture together.

Use this to stuff a joint of pork or serve it as an accompaniment with pork.

Sausage Forcemeat

1 ounce dripping
1 large onion, chopped
1 pound sausagemeat
2 level teaspoons parsley, chopped
1 teaspoon mixed herbs
Grated rind of an orange
2 ounces fresh white breadcrumbs

Melt the dripping in a pan and lightly fry the onion until it is just a golden colour.

Mix the sausagemeat, herbs, orange rind and breadcrumbs together and add the cooked onion. Mix well.

Use with turkey or chicken or as a stuffing for vegetables.

Celery, Tomato and Apple Stuffing

1 ounce butter
1 large onion, chopped
2 sticks of celery, chopped
2 large cooking apples, peeled, cored and
   sliced
6 ounces fresh white breadcrumbs
½ ounce caster sugar
½ teaspoon powdered bay
2 large tomatoes, skinned and chopped

Melt the butter and gently fry the onion
and celery until they are a light golden
colour.

Stir in the sliced apples and cook for a
further 5 minutes.

Mix the breadcrumbs, sugar and bay
together and season well with salt and
pepper.

Add the apple mixture and chopped
tomatoes and mix the ingredients together
thoroughly.

Use with duck or pork – or make a double
quantity for a goose.

Apricot Stuffing

2 ounces butter
1 small onion, chopped
¼ pound dried apricots, soaked for 2 – 3
   hours and drained
6 ounces fresh white breadcrumbs
Juice and grated rind of an orange
A few sprigs of lemon thyme, chopped
2 ounces salted peanuts
1 egg, beaten

Melt the butter in a pan and fry the onion
lightly until it is transparent.

Chop the apricots roughly. Mix together
the breadcrumbs, grated orange rind and
juice, lemon thyme, apricots and salted
peanuts, seasoning well with salt and
pepper.

Add the onion and bind together with
the beaten egg.

Use with duck, goose, pork and lamb.

Nut and Raisin Stuffing

1 ounce butter
1 onion, chopped
2 rashers streaky bacon, chopped
¼ pound fresh white breadcrumbs
2 ounces seedless raisins
2 ounces sultanas
2 ounces walnuts, chopped
1 egg, beaten

Melt the butter and fry the onion gently
until it is transparent, add the bacon and
fry for a further 5 minutes.

Mix the breadcrumbs, dried fruit and
walnuts together. Add the onion and bacon
and mix well.

Season with salt and pepper and bind
with the beaten egg.

Use with poultry, pork and lamb.

Savoury Ham Stuffing

1 ounce butter
4 shallots, chopped
2 ounces mushrooms, chopped
¼ pound ham, chopped
¼ pound fresh white breadcrumbs
A pinch of dry mustard
A pinch of sage
1 egg, beaten

Melt the butter in a pan and fry the shallots gently until they are golden brown.
Add the mushrooms and cook for two
minutes.

Mix the ham and breadcrumbs together,
add the mustard and sage and season with
salt and pepper. Stir in the cooked shallots
and mushrooms and bind with a little
beaten egg.

Use this mixture for stuffing vegetables,
such as onions, marrows and tomatoes.

Fish (Fresh, and Sea Water)

Too often fish cookery is unimaginative: frozen fish fingers for the family, steamed cod for invalids and bought fish and chips for an instant meal – these are sometimes the only guises in which many families encounter fish. Yet fish is a good source of protein and must be unsurpassed in its adaptability. It is equally delicious as a first course, an unusual main dish and as an easily digested food for children.

The waters around this island yield an amazing variety of fish and it is surprising that fish is so often ignored as a constituent for main dishes. Many cooks who are unfamiliar with fish cookery imagine that complicated preparation is necessary but this is not so since even an inexperienced cook will see from these recipes that it is quick and easy to prepare.

Most species of fish have individual and delicious flavours which are best appreciated after being simply cooked, with perhaps the addition of a few herbs. Trout, fresh from the stream if you are lucky enough to catch such a delicacy, is good cooked with fennel, or poached fresh salmon is perfectly complemented by a cucumber dressing. The recipes in this section reflect the regional variations that have developed in cooking fish: Thames eels for Richmond Eel Pie, cider for cooking haddock in South West England, and herrings coated in oatmeal from Scotland. Fish is often thought of as a light meal,

but most housewives are looking for hearty filling food to satisfy the whole family, and country housewives are as aware of this as anyone. However, a fish meal with the right accompaniments can be very sustaining, for example Sage Fish Cakes, or the Tasty Fish Pie. Kedgeree, inherited from the days of elegant and leisurely breakfasts, is a good standby for the modern cook who can give it a country freshness with chopped parsley from the garden.

If you are planning a dinner party then why not include a fish course – tiny crisply fried Whitebait or Red Mullet with Egg Sauce will make a welcome change on your menu.

To obtain the more unusual fish, place a special order with your fishmonger and once you have tasted some of the recipes in this section you will place the order more regularly.

Plaice with Unusual Filling

Serves 4

4 small plaice
1½ ounces butter
¼ pound mushrooms, finely chopped
4 ounces cream cheese
1 ounce fresh white breadcrumbs
1 teaspoon lemon juice
2 teaspoons capers, chopped
1 teaspoon parsley, chopped
½ ounce butter
Lemon wedges

Using a sharp knife remove the fish heads, and cut along the backbone of each plaice on the white side. From this centre cut insert the flat of the blade and loosen the flesh off the bone so that a pocket is formed for the stuffing, but take care not to sever the fillets completely.

Melt the butter in a pan and fry the mushrooms gently. Add the cream cheese, breadcrumbs, lemon juice, capers, parsley and season well with salt and pepper, mixing all the ingredients together thoroughly.

Divide the stuffing into four and press some under each of the loosened fillets, spreading the mixture evenly.

Season the fish well, dot with the remaining butter, and place in the oven at 325°F (Gas Mark 3) for 20 minutes, or until the fish is cooked.

Place on a serving dish, garnish with lemon wedges and serve at once.

Scallops served in their shells

Serves 4

¾ pound potatoes, mashed together with
    ½ ounce butter
1 egg, beaten
1 tablespoon oil
4 rashers back bacon, chopped
8 scallops
1 ounce butter
1 teaspoon lemon juice
Parsley, chopped
Lemon slices

1 piping bag and large star nozzle

Place the mashed potatoes in the piping bag and pipe round the edge of 4 well-scrubbed deep scallop shells, or individual ovenproof dishes. Brush the potato with beaten egg.

Heat the oil in a frying pan and fry the bacon gently for 5 – 7 minutes. Remove the scallops from the flat shells, wash well and drain. Remove the coral and put it on one side, then cut the white part into three or four pieces.

Add the butter to the pan and melt it, then fry the white meat for 3 – 4 minutes. Put the orange coral into the pan and fry for a further 3 minutes, adding the lemon juice and seasoning well with salt and freshly ground pepper.

Place the deep scallop shells under a hot grill to brown the piped potatoes and divide the fish mixture between them.

Sprinkle the parsley over the top of each shell, and garnish with lemon slices. Serve as a snack or first course dish.

Richmond Eel Pie

Serves 4 – 6

2 Thames eels
½ ounce butter
1 large onion, chopped
A large sprig of parsley
Nutmeg, freshly ground
2 glasses dry sherry
2 ounces butter
2 ounces plain flour
Juice of a lemon, strained
2 eggs, hard boiled and cut into quarters
½ pound puff pastry
1 egg, beaten

Skin, bone and clean the eels, then cut them into pieces. Melt the ½ ounce butter in a pan and fry the onion until it is transparent. Add the parsley, nutmeg, salt and freshly ground pepper and sherry. Bring to the boil and add the eels, simmering for 10 minutes. Remove the eels to a pie dish and strain the liquor.

To make the sauce, melt the 2 ounces butter in a pan, stir in the flour and cook for 2 minutes, gradually mixing in the strained liquor. Bring to the boil and cook for 5 minutes, adding the lemon juice and seasoning with salt and pepper if necessary.

Arrange the egg quarters on top of the eels in the pie dish and pour the sauce over them, allowing it to cool.

Roll out the pastry and cover the pie dish in the usual way. Brush with beaten egg. Bake at 425°F (Gas Mark 5) for a further 15 – 20 minutes. Serve either hot or cold.

Grilled Red Mullet with Egg Sauce

Serves 4

4 red mullet
2 lemons, sliced thinly
1 small onion, chopped
¼ pint port wine
½ pint egg sauce (see page 20)

Clean the mullet, but do not gut them. Score the fish 3 or 4 times diagonally on each side, and place them in a flat dish.

Arrange the lemon and onion on top of the fish, season with salt and freshly ground black pepper and pour in the port wine. Allow the mullet to stand in the wine mixture for at least 4 hours, turning several times.

Drain the fish and place on a grill pan. Grill for 10 minutes on each side, brushing on some of the port mixture from time to time.

Serve at once with the egg sauce.

Fresh Salmon and Cucumber Dressing

Serves 6

2 pounds Scotch salmon
3 pints chicken stock
1 bayleaf
1 large cucumber, diced
¼ pint chicken stock
1 ounce butter
1 ounce plain flour
1 pint milk
2 tablespoons double cream
Lemon slices

Poach the salmon in the chicken stock with the bayleaf, salt and pepper for 20 minutes, or until the fish is cooked through.

Cover the cucumber with the ¼ pint of chicken stock and bring to the boil. After simmering for 5 minutes press the cucumber through a sieve.

Melt the butter in a pan, stir in the flour, and cook for 2 minutes. Gradually add the milk and bring to the boil, stirring constantly. Add the cucumber mixture and season well with salt and pepper.

Drain the salmon, remove the skin and divide the fish into 6 portions. Arrange this on a serving dish and keep warm.

Add the cream to the cucumber sauce and serve with the salmon. Garnish with lemon slices.

A Tasty Fish Pie

Serves 4 – 6

2 pounds haddock, cooked
2 ounces butter
3 tablespoons plain flour
½ pint milk
½ teaspoon anchovy essence
2 tablespoons parsley, chopped
4 tablespoons Cheddar cheese, grated
½ ounce butter
1 tablespoon cream or milk
1½ pound potatoes, cooked and mashed

Remove all the skin and bones from the haddock, and flake it finely. Make a sauce by melting the butter in a pan, stirring in the flour and cooking for 2 minutes. Gradually stir in the milk, bring to the boil and cook for 3 minutes. Season with salt and pepper, anchovy essence, parsley and half the grated cheese. Stir in the flaked fish and put into a buttered ovenproof dish.

Beat the butter and cream into the mashed potatoes, and pile this mixture on top of the fish, sprinkling the remaining cheese over the top. Bake at 375°F (Gas Mark 5) for 25 minutes or until golden brown. Serve at once.

Whitebait as prepared at Greenwich

Serves 6

2 pounds whitebait
¼ pound plain flour
Oil for frying
Lemon wedges

A paper bag or polythene bag

Wash the whitebait in salted water, and dry thoroughly. Place the flour in a paper or polythene bag and season well with salt and pepper. Toss the whitebait in the seasoned flour until each one is well coated. Shake off the surplus flour.

Heat the oil in a pan to 375°F and fry the whitebait in this until they are lightly browned and crisp. Drain on absorbent paper. Serve very hot with lemon wedges.

Amberley Trout

Serves 6

6 Trout
Fennel, finely chopped
¼ pint white wine
1 ounce butter

Season the trout with salt and freshly ground black pepper. Place the fish in a buttered ovenproof dish and sprinkle generously with fennel leaves.

Moisten with white wine, cover with a lid or aluminium foil and bake at 350°F (Gas Mark 4) for 25 minutes, or until the trout is cooked through.

Remove the fish to a serving dish. Reduce the liquor and thicken with the butter. Adjust the seasoning and pour over the trout. Serve at once.

Turbot with Horseradish Cream

Serves 4

2 pounds turbot
1 tablespoon flour
A pinch of cayenne pepper
1 tablespoon dehydrated horseradish
2 tablespoons water
1 small onion, chopped very finely
¼ pound button mushrooms, sliced
2 ounces peeled prawns
½ pint double cream

Remove the dark skin from the turbot and cut the fish into four pieces. Wash and drain on absorbent paper, and season with salt and pepper then coat with the flour. Sprinkle the cayenne pepper over each piece and place the fish in a buttered ovenproof dish.

Blend the horseradish and water together and spread it over the fish. Sprinkle the onion and mushrooms over the top and add the prawns. Pour in the cream and cover the dish with a lid or aluminium foil.

Bake at 400°F, (Gas Mark 6) for 30 – 35 minutes. Serve at once.

Kedgeree

Serves 4

4 ounces long grain rice
2 large eggs
1 pound smoked haddock
½ pint milk or water
2 ounces butter
3 tablespoons parsley, chopped

Cook the rice in boiling salted water for
11 – 12 minutes and drain well. Boil the
eggs for 10 minutes, cool immediately under
running cold water and then remove the
shells.

Poach the smoked haddock in a shallow
frying pan with the milk for 10 – 12 minutes,
or until it is cooked. Strain, remove bones
and skin then flake the fish roughly with a
fork. Melt the butter in a pan and toss the
rice and fish together. Chop the eggs and
add these with half the parsley and plenty
of salt and pepper. Heat the mixture
thoroughly and pile the kedgeree
into a hot serving dish. Garnish with the
remaining parsley and serve at once.

Herrings in Oatmeal

Serves 4

4 herrings
6 tablespoons coarse oatmeal
Oil for frying
Lemon wedges

Scrape the herrings from tail to head on
both sides under running water. Cut off the
heads, gut, remove the fins and wash again.
Dry the fish to remove excess moisture.

Season the oatmeal with salt and freshly
ground pepper and use this to coat the
herrings. Fry them in the oil in a large
skillet for about 15 minutes or until they
are brown and cooked through.

Serve with lemon wedges.

Herrings Stuffed with Mustard Butter

Serves 4

4 herrings
3 ounces butter
1 teaspoon English mustard

Split the herrings open lengthways, remove
the backbones and open out each fish so
that it lies flat. Cream the butter, mustard,
salt and freshly ground pepper, then
spread this mixture all over the inside of
the herrings and fold them back into shape
again.

Wrap each one in aluminium foil and put
the parcels on a baking sheet. Cook at
375°F (Gas Mark 5) for 25 minutes, or until
the fish are tender.

Serve with brown bread and butter.

Sage Fish Cakes

Serves 4

¾ pound cod, cooked
1 pound potatoes, freshly cooked
1 ounce butter
1 egg, beaten
2 tablespoons single cream
1 tablespoon sage, chopped
1 egg, beaten
4 – 5 tablespoons bread crumbs
Oil for frying

Flake the fish finely using a fork. Mash the potatoes and mix with the cod. Add the butter, egg, cream and sage then season with salt and pepper.

Make the mixture into a roll and divide it into eight even-sized pieces. Shape each one into a round and dip the fish cakes into the beaten egg, and then press on the crumbs to form a coating, and shake off any surplus.

Heat the oil in a large frying pan and fry the cakes until they are golden brown. Drain on absorbent paper.

Serve the fish cakes hot with a parsley or egg sauce. (see page 20)

Mackerel with Gooseberry Sauce

Serves 4

4 medium sized mackerel
2 tablespoons lemon juice
1 ounce butter
Gooseberry Sauce – (see page 21)

Cut off the mackerel heads and gut the fish. Remove the fins and trim the tails. Wash the fish thoroughly and season with salt and freshly ground pepper. Squeeze the lemon juice over them and dot with butter.

Grill the mackerel for 8 – 10 minutes on each side, or until the fish is cooked through. Serve with hot gooseberry sauce.

Orchard Haddock

Serves 4

1½ pound haddock fillets
1 onion, sliced
1 bayleaf
2 Bramley cooking apples, peeled and
   sliced
½ pint dry cider
1 tablespoon fresh breadcrumbs
3 ounces Cheddar cheese, grated
Watercress

Cut the haddock into large pieces and place in a buttered ovenproof dish with the sliced onion, bayleaf and apples. Pour in the cider and season well with salt and freshly ground pepper. Cover with a lid or aluminium foil, and bake at 375°F (Gas Mark 5) for 25 minutes.

Remove the dish from the oven, mix the breadcrumbs and cheese together and sprinkle these over the top. Place under a preheated grill for 5 – 8 minutes, or until golden brown. Garnish with watercress, and serve at once.

Meat, Poultry and Game

This is the longest section in the book since most meals have meat for the main course. Therefore the recipes reflect a wide variety of regional specialities. Throughout the country the choice of meat is the same, but pork cooked in the South of England would possibly taste quite different when prepared and eaten in the North, and these recipes show how housewives developed their differing styles of cookery. Sometimes a change of cooking liquor, cider instead of stock, different herbs such as rosemary and thyme instead of sage, or an alternative method of cooking will help to identify the origin of a recipe.

Economy was as important to the country housewife long ago as it is to everyone today, and a dislike of waste compelled the country women to devise appetising and interesting ways of cooking and using the entire carcase. In this section you will find recipes for using oxtail, liver, hearts and ox tongue all of which are delicious when you prepare them yourself, and are much easier to do than most people imagine.

The most plentiful meat available to country families was poultry, or the proceeds from the hunter's bag. And though the modern housewife is unlikely to be cooking game that has been shot by the family or friends it is possible to buy hare, rabbit and game birds in season so you need not miss a marvellous meal of Poacher's Pie or Harvest-time Pheasant.

The chief problem for farmers' wives,

and one that is shared by every mother, is to have a hot meal ready for her family when they come home. Roasts and grills do not improve with keeping warm, but casseroles can be kept waiting. These dishes make use of the cheaper cuts of meat and produce tasty, nourishing meals. Jugged Hare, Chicken in cider, Ada Tingle's Chicken Casserole and Hunter's Beef in Beer will all prove as popular with today's families as they did with hungry farm workers and hunting parties.

Country cooking counsels economy, so make a little meat go a long way in recipes such as Steak and Kidney Pudding or Steak and Mushroom Pie, or add suet dumplings to a stew and the family will not even miss the meat.

Pork with Rosemary and Lemon

Serves 4

4 pork chump chops
2 lemons
3 teaspoons fresh rosemary, chopped
1 onion, chopped finely
2 ounces mushrooms, sliced
1 ounce butter

Aluminium foil

Trim the chops and place each one on a piece of aluminium foil. Grate the lemons and sprinkle the rind over each chop, also adding the fresh rosemary.

Season well with salt and pepper and cover each chop with the onion and mushrooms, then dot with butter.

Fold over and seal the aluminium foil so that the meat is enclosed. Place the four packages in a baking tray and bake at 400°F (Gas Mark 6) for 30 – 35 minutes, or until the meat is tender.

Somerset Pork

Serves 4

2 tablespoons oil
2 large onions, sliced into rings
1¼ pounds pork fillet
½ ounce seasoned flour
¼ pound mushrooms, sliced
A sprig of rosemary
½ pound prunes, soaked overnight
½ pint beef stock
¼ pint soured cream
1 tablespoon parsley, chopped

Heat the oil in a pan and fry the onions until they are transparent. Trim the pork and cut into 1 inch slices. Toss the meat in the seasoned flour and fry until it is browned on all sides.

Place the onions and meat in a shallow casserole dish, add the mushrooms, rosemary and prunes, then season well with salt and pepper. Pour in the stock, cover and cook at 375°F (Gas Mark 5) for 55 minutes – 1 hour.

Remove the casserole from the oven, stir in the cream and return to the oven for a further 5 minutes. Serve with mashed potatoes.

Autumn Pork Chops

Serves 4

4 lean pork chops
1 large onion, sliced into rings
2 Bramley cooking apples, cored, peeled
  and sliced
4 ounces mushrooms
2 tablespoons tomato purée
¼ pint white wine or stock
1 medium-sized can tomatoes

Trim the chops and wipe them. Place a
layer of onions in the base of a casserole
dish, followed by half the apples and
mushrooms.

Put the chops in next, season well with
salt and pepper, then cover them with the
remaining onions, apples and mushrooms.
Blend the tomato purée with the wine or
stock and pour this mixture over the chops.
Add the tomatoes and cook at 350°F (Gas
Mark 4) for 1¼ hours or until the chops are
tender.

Hunter's Beef in Beer

Serves 6

4 pounds brisket of beef
½ pound back bacon, chopped
1 pound onions, sliced into rings
½ pound carrots, chopped
½ pint brown ale
½ pint rich beef stock
¼ pint vinegar
A bunch of herbs
¼ pound mushrooms, sliced

Roll up the brisket and secure it with
string. Place the meat in a casserole dish,
add the bacon, onions and carrots.

Heat the brown ale, stock and vinegar in
a pan and pour this over the meat. Add the
bunch of herbs and season with salt and
pepper.

Cover with a lid and cook for 3½ hours
300°F (Gas Mark 2). Remove from the oven,
add the mushrooms, adjust the seasoning
if necessary and return to the oven for a
further 15 minutes.

Serve with mashed potatoes and green
vegetables.

Chicken with Lemon and Honey
A fresh taste for Chicken

Serves 4

4 chicken joints
2 ounces butter
Juice and grated rind of a lemon
Juice and grated rind of an orange
4 level tablespoons honey
Fresh rosemary, chopped
Parsley, chopped
Lemon wedges

Trim the chicken joints and fry in the
butter until the chicken is golden brown,
then cover and cook for 25 minutes, or
until the chicken is cooked through.

Add the juice and rind of the lemon and
orange, then stir in the honey and rosemary, seasoning well with salt and freshly
ground black pepper.

Bring to the boil and baste the chicken
well with the sauce. Place the chicken on a
serving dish, pour the sauce over it and
garnish with chopped parsley and lemon
wedges.

Tripe and Onions

Serves 4 – 6

2 large onions, chopped
2 pounds dressed tripe
1 pint milk
2 ounces butter
2 ounces plain flour
Parsley, chopped

Place the onion in a pan, cover with water
and simmer for 10 – 15 minutes. Cut the
tripe into eight portions and add this to the
pan, seasoning well with salt and pepper.
Simmer for a further 30 minutes.

Add most of the milk and butter and
bring to the boil, then cream the remaining
milk with the flour and add this to the pan,
stirring continually. Adjust the seasoning
to taste and sprinkle with parsley. Serve
with mashed potatoes.

Cornish Pasties

Serves 4

12 ounces shortcrust pastry
¾ pound potatoes, thinly sliced
½ pound onions, thinly sliced
½ ounce butter
¾ pound chuck or skirt steak
1 egg, beaten

A round plate 9 inches in diameter
A pastry brush

Roll out the pastry and cut into 4 rounds using the plate as a guide. Put these on one side. Arrange the potato down the centre of each pastry round, and cover with onion, season with salt and pepper and dot with butter. Dice the meat finely and arrange it on top of the vegetables.

Dampen the edges of each pastry round, and draw the edges together on top of the filling to enclose it completely. Crimp the edges together using the finger and thumb.

Put the pasties on a baking sheet and brush over with beaten egg. Bake at 400°F, (Gas Mark 6) for 40 minutes, then reduce the temperature to 350°F (Gas Mark 3) for a further 20 minutes. Serve either hot or cold.

Scotch Collops

Serves 4

1 ounce dripping
1 large onion, chopped
1 pound freshly minced beef
1 tablespoon mixed herbs
2 tablespoons oatmeal
About ¼ pint stock

Melt the dripping in a pan and lightly fry the onion until it is golden brown. Add the mince and brown it all over.

Season very well with salt and pepper and stir in the mixed herbs. Sprinkle in the oatmeal and sufficient stock to moisten the mixture. Cover and simmer for 30 – 40 minutes.

Pile into a serving dish and serve with mashed potatoes and swedes.

Liver Hot Pot

Serves 4

1 large onion, sliced into rings
2 carrots, chopped
2 sticks of celery, chopped
2 tablespoons seasoned flour
1 pound ox liver, sliced and soaked for several hours in milk
1 medium-sized can tomatoes
1½ pounds potatoes, sliced
1 ounce butter
A small quantity of stock

Toss the vegetables in the seasoned flour and place half of them in a greased casserole dish, seasoning well with salt and pepper.

Toss the liver in the seasoned flour and place this in the casserole dish. Cover it with the rest of the mixed vegetables and season again.

Pour in the tomatoes and mix them with the vegetables. Arrange the sliced potatoes on top and dot them with the butter.

Moisten with a little stock and bake 350°F (Gas Mark 4) for 45 minutes – 1 hour, or until the vegetables are cooked.

Oxtail Brawn

Serves 4

1 oxtail
½ pound leg of beef or skirt
2 onions, cut in half
A bunch of herbs
4 cloves
4 peppercorns
¼ pint dry red wine
2 bayleaves
Water
Watercress

A 1 – 1½ pint pudding basin or mould
A piece of muslin

Trim the fat from the oxtail and beef, and cut into pieces. Put the meat in a pan, cover it with water, bring to the boil and simmer for 15 minutes. Strain off the water and return the meat to the pan, together with the onions.

Place the herbs, cloves and peppercorns on the piece of muslin and tie them up. Add this, the wine and bayleaves and just enough water to cover the ingredients.

Bring to the boil and simmer for 4 hours, or until the meat is tender. Allow to cool then remove the meat from the bones, and place it in the mould or pudding basin.

Strain the stock over the meat and leave in a refrigerator to set. Turn out onto a serving dish and garnish with watercress.

Poacher's Pie

Serves 6

1 rabbit
1 ounce seasoned flour
1 ounce butter
1 onion, sliced
¾ pound bacon, diced
2 eggs, hard boiled
2 ounces mushrooms, sliced
½ pint chicken stock
½ pound shortcrust or puff pastry

1 pie dish

Cut the rabbit into small joints and toss these in seasoned flour. Fry the meat in the melted butter until it is brown, and arrange the pieces in layers with the onions and bacon, seasoning well with salt and pepper. Cut the hard boiled eggs in quarters and arrange them on top of the meat.

Place the mushrooms on top and pour in the stock. Cover with pastry in the usual way, and bake at 425°F (Gas Mark 7) for 45 minutes. Reduce the temperature to 375°F (Gas Mark 5), cover the pastry with grease-proof paper and cook for a further 20 – 25 minutes. Serve hot or cold.

Steak and Kidney Pudding

Serves 4

¾ pound chuck or skirt steak
2 – 3 ounces pig's kidney
1 large onion, sliced into rings
Stock or water
Pastry:
6 ounces self-raising flour
½ level teaspoon salt
1½ ounces shredded suet
¼ pint cold water (just under)

A 2 pint pudding basin, greased
Greaseproof paper, string and scissors
A steamer

Trim the steak and kidney and cut into
1 inch pieces, seasoning the meat well with
salt and pepper.

Sift the flour and salt into a bowl, stir in
the suet and mix to a soft dough with the
cold water. Turn it onto a well-floured
pastry board and knead lightly.

Cut off a quarter of the dough for the lid
and put aside. Shape the rest into a round
and roll out to the size of a dinner plate.
Dust it lightly with flour, fold into four and
carefully lift it into the pudding basin.
Gently unfold the pastry and press it evenly
into the sides of the basin, allowing a ½ inch
overlap at the top.

Fill the pudding with the meat and onion,
adding 3 tablespoons of stock. Roll out the
remaining pastry to fit the top of the basin,
dampen the edges and press the two pieces
together.

Make a pleat in a piece of greaseproof
paper and tie it over the pudding, leaving
the fold in position. Make a handle with the
string, so that the basin can be lifted easily.

Steam the pudding for 6 hours, either in
a steamer or in a saucepan.

Remove the string and greaseproof paper.
Make a small hole in the pastry lid and
pour in some boiling stock to increase the
gravy. Wrap a napkin around the basin and
serve the pudding with mashed potatoes
and a green vegetable.

Cumberland Ring

Serves 4 – 6

¾ pound pork sausagemeat
1 pound rough puff or puff pastry
Parsley and sage, chopped
1 egg, beaten

A pastry brush

Place the sausagemeat on a well-floured
pastry board, and roll it into a long strip
approximately a ¼ inch thick and 20 inches
long. Roll out the pastry making it slightly
longer than the sausagemeat and about 4½
inches wide. Lay the sausagemeat down the
centre of the pastry and sprinkle it with the
chopped herbs.

Brush the pastry with beaten egg, and
fold its edges over so that they join evenly,
then press them together. Turn the roll so
that the joined edge is underneath.

Lift the roll carefully onto a baking sheet
and shape it into a circle, pressing the two
ends firmly together. Using scissors, make
small slits every inch all round it.

Brush the ring with beaten egg and bake
at 425°F (Gas Mark 7) for 30 – 35 minutes, or
until the pastry is golden brown. Use two
fish slices to remove the ring to a serving
dish. Serve hot or cold.

Ox Tongue with Mustard Sauce

Serves 4 – 6

1 ox tongue (already boned by the butcher)
6 peppercorns
2 large onions
3 carrots
2 stalks celery
A bunch of herbs
Mustard sauce (see page 20)
Stock or water

Soak the tongue in cold water for 1 – 2 hours and then drain well. Place it in a large pan and add the peppercorns, vegetables, bunch of herbs, salt and pepper. Cover with beef stock or water, bring to the boil, remove any scum and simmer for 3 – 3½ hours, or until the tongue is tender.

Allow the meat to cool slightly in the stock, then strain off the liquid, remove all the bones and fat from the root of the tongue and peel off the skin, using a clean cloth to hold the hot meat.

Place the tongue on a hot serving dish, and serve with leaf spinach, boiled potatoes and the mustard sauce.

The remaining tongue is delicious served cold with jacket potatoes and pickles.

Crown Roast of Lamb

Serves 4 – 6

2 best end joints of lamb, chopped and
    skinned, eight cutlets on each
½ ounce butter
1½ ounces onions, finely chopped
2 ounces mushrooms
¼ pound sausagemeat
1 clove garlic, crushed
2 tablespoons parsley, chopped
2 ounces fresh white breadcrumbs
¼ pound dried apricots, soaked overnight
    and chopped
1 egg, beaten
1 ounce butter, melted
2 pounds potatoes, creamed
Parsley
Stock or water

A trussing needle and fine string
A pastry brush
A piping bag and large star nozzle
16 cutlet frills

Remove most of the fat from the meat, and trim the rib bones to an equal length. Scrape the top inch of each bone free of meat, place the two joints back to back, skinned sides facing, and sew the joint ends together using a trussing needle and fine string. Place the crown on a roasting tray.

Prepare the stuffing by melting the butter in a pan and frying the onions gently until they are transparent. Add the mushrooms and cook for 2 minutes, then turn the mixture into a bowl and add the sausagemeat, garlic, parsley, breadcrumbs and chopped apricots. Season well with salt and pepper and mix thoroughly.

Moisten the mixture with the beaten egg and fill the crown tightly with the stuffing.

Cover the bone tips with aluminium foil to prevent charring, and brush the melted butter over the meat with a pastry brush.

Roast the meat at 350°F (Gas Mark 4) for 1½ – 2 hours, or until tender. Remove the foil from the bone tips and cover them with the cutlet frills. Place the meat on a hot serving dish and garnish with piped potato and parsley.

Welsh Lamb Casserole

Serves 6

2 pound leg of lamb
2 ounces butter
1 pound leeks, washed and cut into slices
¼ pound mushrooms
1 lemon
A pinch of rosemary
¼ pint chicken stock
½ ounce butter
1 tablespoon plain flour

Roast the lamb at 350°F (Gas Mark 4) for about 1½ hours. Allow to cool, then cut off the excess fat.

Melt the butter in a pan and fry the leeks until they are transparent. Add the mushrooms and cook for a further 5 minutes. Place the lamb in a large casserole dish and put the vegetables round it.

Carefully remove the peel from the lemon, cut it into strips and add this with the lemon juice to the casserole. Season with salt, pepper and rosemary, then pour in the stock, cover and cook for 1½ hours at 300°F (Gas Mark 2).

Place the lamb on a serving dish and keep it hot. Melt the ½ ounce of butter in a pan, stir in the flour and cook for 2 minutes. Add the stock and vegetables, bring to the boil, stirring continually and cook for 3 minutes. Pour the vegetable sauce over the lamb and serve at once.

Steak and Mushroom Pie

Serves 4

1½ pounds skirt of beef
2 ounces ox kidney
1 ounce seasoned flour
1 ounce dripping
2 large onions, sliced into rings
¼ pint dry red wine
¼ pint beef stock
A bunch of herbs
½ pound button mushrooms, sliced
½ pound shortcrust pastry
1 egg, beaten

A 2 pint pie dish
A pie funnel

Trim the meat and cut into 1 inch dice. Remove the core and cut up the kidney. Toss the meat in the seasoned flour. Melt the dripping in a pan and fry the onions gently until they are transparent. Add the meat and fry until it is browned all over.

Pour in the wine and stock, add the herbs and season well with salt and pepper. Bring to the boil and simmer for 1½ – 2 hours, or until the meat is tender. Add the mushrooms and mix well.

Transfer the meat to a 2 pint pie dish, place the funnel in the centre and allow the meat to cool.

Roll out the pastry and place it on top of the dish, fluting the edges and brushing with beaten egg. Bake at 425°F (Gas Mark 7) for 25 minutes or until the pastry is golden brown. Serve hot.

Ada Tingle's Chicken Casserole

Serves 6

1½ ounces butter
2 large onions, sliced into rings
1 x 3 pound chicken
1 medium sized can tomatoes
½ pint dry cider
A bunch of herbs
2 tablespoons tomato purée
2 tablespoons cornflour
1 tablespoon water

Melt the butter in a pan and fry the onion gently until it is transparent, then drain well, and place in a casserole dish. Fry the chicken on all sides until it is golden brown, and put that in the casserole dish adding the canned tomatoes, cider, bunch of herbs, tomato purée, salt and pepper.

Cover and cook for 1½ hours at 375°F (Gas Mark 5), or until the chicken is tender. Strain the tomato stock into a pan, blend the cornflour with the water and stir it into the stock. Bring to the boil and simmer for 2 minutes stirring all the time. Pour this sauce over the chicken and serve at once.

Love in Disguise

Serves 4

4 sheep's hearts
2 ounces dried apricots
¼ pound fresh breadcrumbs
1 onion, chopped finely
1 teaspoon rosemary, chopped
1 ounce butter, softened

Soak the hearts in salted water for half an hour to remove the blood. Cut out the tubes carefully and remove the division in the middle of the heart with a sharp knife. Dry thoroughly.

Drain the apricots and cut them up. Mix the pieces with the breadcrumbs, onion, rosemary, salt and pepper, and blend in the butter. Fill the hearts with this stuffing and sew them up with cotton.

Place the hearts on a greased baking sheet and bake at 400°F (Gas Mark 6) for 40 – 45 minutes, basting frequently. Serve with redcurrant jelly.

Duck with Grape Stuffing

Serves 4 – 6

1 x 5 pound duck, with giblets
1 tablespoon dripping
1 large onion, chopped
¼ pound mushrooms, chopped
3 ounces fresh white breadcrumbs
Juice and rind of a small orange
1 teaspoon lemon juice
6 ounces black grapes, cut in half
    with pips removed
2 ounces shelled walnuts, chopped
1 teaspoon parsley, chopped
1 teaspoon mixed herbs
1 tablespoon redcurrant jelly
1 small orange

Remove the giblets, wash them and place in a pan covered with water, bringing them to the boil and simmering for about 1 hour. This stock may be used to make the gravy.

Melt the dripping and fry the onion gently until it is transparent. Stir in the mushrooms and cook for a further 2 minutes.

Place the breadcrumbs in a mixing bowl, together with the rind and juice of the orange, the lemon juice and the grapes.

Add the onions, mushrooms, walnuts and herbs, seasoning well with salt and pepper. Dissolve the redcurrant jelly in a pan and add this to the mixture.

Wash and wipe the duck and fill it with the stuffing, folding the flap of skin over the tail. Prick the duck all over with a fork and place it in a roasting tin. Roast for 1½ hours, or until it is golden brown and thoroughly cooked.

Remove the bird to a hot serving dish, pouring off most of the fat and making a gravy in the usual way with the giblet stock.

Slice the other orange and arrange it around the bird.

Serve with a selection of fresh vegetables.

Beef Olives

Serves 4

4 thin slices topside
4 rashers back bacon
2 ounces fresh breadcrumbs
A pinch of parsley, chopped
A pinch of sage, chopped
A pinch of thyme, chopped
1 egg, beaten
2 ounces dripping
1 onion, sliced
1 carrot, diced
1 stick of celery, chopped
A bunch of herbs
1 ounce flour

Trim the steak and flatten with a rolling pin, seasoning well with salt and pepper. Place a rasher of bacon on each piece of beef.

Mix the breadcrumbs, herbs, salt and freshly ground pepper together and mix to a stiff consistency with beaten egg.

Divide the stuffing into four and spread each part on one of the slices. Roll up the beef olives and secure with string or cocktail sticks.

Melt the dripping in a pan and fry the vegetables until they are tender. Lay the beef olives on top of the vegetables, add the bunch of herbs and cook for 1½ hours or until the meat is tender.

After removing the string or cocktail sticks place the beef olives on a serving dish and keep them hot. Add the flour to the vegetable mixture, cook for 2 minutes and pour this over the beef olives. Serve with rice or mashed potatoes.

Yorkshire Bacon

Serves 4 – 6

A piece of bacon
2 ounces dripping
2 onions, sliced into rings
4 carrots, sliced
1 turnip, diced
2 sticks of celery, sliced
1½ pints dry cider
A bunch of herbs

Soak the bacon for 1 hour in cold water and drain well. Melt the dripping in a pan and fry the onions until they are transparent. Add the carrots, turnip and celery and fry for a further 10 minutes. Put the vegetables in a casserole dish.

Place the bacon on top of them and pour in the cider, adding the bunch of herbs and seasoning with salt and pepper. Cover the casserole dish with a lid, and place in the oven at 350°F (Gas Mark 4), allowing 20 – 25 minutes a pound according to the size of the joint. Half an hour before it is cooked, remove the bacon rind and continue cooking with the casserole uncovered.

The cider stock and vegetables can be thickened with cornflour, or the ham can be served with parsley sauce. (see page 20)

Jugged Hare

Serves 4 – 6

1 hare
¼ pound lean bacon
2 ounces dripping
2 onions, sliced into rings
1 carrot, chopped
A bunch of herbs
1 pint beef stock
1½ ounces plain flour
¼ pint port wine
1 tablespoon redcurrant jelly
Parsley, chopped

Cut the hare into joints and wipe well. Chop the bacon and fry this and the hare joints in the melted dripping until it is all browned.

Add the vegetables and the bunch of herbs, then season well with salt and pepper. Pour in the stock, bring to the boil and simmer for 1½ hours, or until the hare is tender.

Mix the flour with the port wine and add to the pan with the redcurrant jelly, return the contents to the boil and simmer for a further ½ hour.

Place the hare on a hot serving dish and pour the sauce over it. Serve at once garnished with chopped parsley.

Harvest-time Pheasant

Serves 4

2 pheasants
2 ounces dripping
1 pound onions, sliced into rings
4 sticks of celery, chopped
¼ pound streaky bacon, chopped
1 pound Bramley cooking apples, peeled,
    cored and cut in thick slices
A bunch of fresh herbs
½ pint dry cider

Wipe the pheasants inside and out. Melt
the dripping in a pan and fry the onion and
celery lightly until they are a golden colour.
Add the bacon and cook for a further 2
minutes then remove from the pan.

Fry the pheasants on all sides in the
remaining dripping until they are golden
brown.

Put half of the onion mixture in a casserole dish and place the pheasants on top,
with the apples arranged all round the
birds.

Add the bunch or herbs, season well with
salt and pepper and pour in the cider.

Cook at 325°F (Gas Mark 3) for approximately 2 hours, or until the pheasants are
very tender.

Oxtail Stew, full of Dumplings

Serves 4 – 6

1 large oxtail
1 ounce dripping
½ pound onions, sliced thickly
½ pound carrots, sliced thickly
2 leeks, cut into 1 inch pieces
1 ounce flour
1½ pints beef stock
½ pint cheap red wine
1 tablespoon tomato purée (optional)
A bunch of fresh herbs
1 tablespoon lemon juice
Dumplings:
2 – 3 ounces beef dripping
½ pound self raising flour
A pinch of salt
1 level teaspoon baking powder
A small quantity of water

Divide the oxtail into joints, wipe and dry
them well. Melt the dripping in a large pan
and fry the oxtail gently before adding the
vegetables, frying for 5 minutes then
stirring in the flour and mixing well. Pour
the beef stock and red wine into the pan
and bring to the boil, simmering it, under a
cover, for 1 – 1½ hours.

Strain off the liquid and allow it to cool
completely, then remove the fat from it
with a metal spoon. Put the meat and
vegetables into a casserole dish with the
tomato purée, the bunch of herbs and lemon
juice. Cover the pan and cook at 300°F
(Gas Mark 2) for 2½ hours.

To make the dumplings, rub the dripping
into the dry ingredients and add sufficient
water to make a soft dough. Using floured
hands divide the dough into eight dumplings.

Increase the oven temperature to 375°F
(Gas Mark 5). Arrange the dumplings on
top of the casserole and cook for a further
½ hour, or until the dumplings are fluffy
and cooked.

Vegetables

The essence of good country cooking is to prepare the freshest foods in the simplest way. Obviously this maxim can be applied to any field of cookery, but it is in dealing with vegetables that it is most important. Any fresh young produce from the garden will need only a little cooking in a small amount of water, and a knob of butter on top before serving. It would be sacrilege to destroy the flavour of tiny peas, small carrots, beetroots the size of walnuts, new potatoes and young runner beans with prolonged cooking.

However, it is possible to want a change from plain vegetables and the recipes in this section should give you plenty of ideas for new ways of serving them. Several of the dishes, such as Baked Onions with Country Stuffing and Shropshire Fidget Pie, make a light meal in themselves; and the flavours of the carrot and leek dish or Elsie Eaton's Special Cabbage are well worth trying. Traditional favourites like Pease Pudding and Bubble and Squeak may have been forgotten, but once they are revived they will soon be re-established as favourites with the whole family.

Potatoes have always been the main-stay of country cooking because they were easily available for most of the year and cheap. They also make a satisfying change from bread as you will see from the recipe for Potato Scones; serve these for an excellent breakfast with bacon and eggs. A filling snack in the true country style is a baked potato – just pop two or three in the oven when you are making another dish and cook until soft, cut in half and serve very hot with lots of butter and a topping of grated cheese.

When writing of country vegetables it is impossible to ignore the wide range of salad plants that have so much more flavour when freshly gathered from the garden. The people of this country have always had a passion for gardening – and a revival is under way now, with the trend towards the vegetable patch rather than the flower border – so it should be possible, even in smallest garden, to tuck a few lettuces amongst the flowers, or raise a row of colourful scarlet runner beans beside the hedge. Little sweet radishes, crispy lettuces that haven't had time to wilt in the shops, small, slightly bitter ridge cucumbers and tomatoes – even the tiny ones that can be grown out of doors – have a delicious flavour which is perhaps only a childhood memory to you. To give real country style and colour to a salad add a few marigold or nasturtium petals and chopped tarragon leaves or sprigs of mint.

An Unusual Dish of Carrots and Leeks

Serves 4 – 6

1 ounce butter
1 pound carrots, sliced
2 pints stock
1½ pound leeks, chopped
¼ pint soured cream

Melt the butter in a pan and fry the carrots gently without browning them. Pour in the stock, season with salt and pepper, bring to the boil and cook for 25 minutes or until the carrots are tender.

Add the leeks, return to the boil and simmer for a further 8 – 10 minutes. Drain the carrots and leeks well and return them to the pan. Pour the soured cream over the vegetables, season with black pepper, bring to boiling point and serve immediately.

Shropshire Fidget Pie

Serves 4 – 6

1 pound potatoes, peeled and sliced ⅛ inch thick
½ pound Bramley apples, peeled, cored and sliced
½ pound back bacon, chopped
1 tablespoon demerara sugar
¼ pint stock
2 tablespoons tomato purée
½ pound shortcrust pastry
1 egg, beaten

A 2 pint pie dish
A pie funnel

Arrange the potatoes, apples and bacon in layers in the pie dish, seasoning well with salt and pepper.

Sprinkle the demerara sugar over these and add the stock and tomato purée, after blending them together. Place the pie funnel in the centre of the dish.

Roll out the pastry and cover the pie filling, flute the edges and brush all over the top with beaten egg.

Bake at 400°F (Gas Mark 6) for 1¼ – 1½ hours. (If the pastry gets too brown, cover with greaseproof paper and continue cooking.)

Pudding in the Corner

Serves 4 – 6

¼ pound self-raising flour
¼ pound shredded suet
A pinch of salt
1 large onion, chopped
A small quantity of water

Place the flour, suet and salt in a mixing bowl with the onion and stir well.

Add sufficient water to make a stiff paste, and spread this 1½ inches thick in a greased roasting tin. Bake at 350°F (Gas Mark 4) for 45 – 50 minutes, or until the pudding is crisp and golden brown.

Crofter's Herb Pudding

Serves 4 – 6

2 ounces pearl barley
1 pound spring cabbage, chopped
¼ pound nettles, chopped
2 onions, chopped
2 leeks, sliced
1 ounce butter
1 egg
1 tablespoon mixed herbs

A 2 pint ovenproof dish

Soak the barley overnight in 1 pint of cold water. Next day boil the barley in this water for about 40 minutes until it is tender.

Place the vegetables in a large saucepan, add the barley and the cooking liquid with sufficient water to cover the vegetables. Season well with salt and pepper.

Bring to the boil, and cook rapidly for 20-25 minutes. Drain well and return the vegetables to the pan.

Add the butter, egg and herbs, stirring well. Turn the mixture into the dish, cover and bake at 350°F (Gas Mark 4) for 15 minutes. Serve hot as a supper dish, or with cold meats.

Cornish Leek Pie

Serves 4 – 6

1 pound leeks, cut in 1 inch pieces
½ pint white sauce (see page 20)
1 pound potatoes, peeled
1 ounce butter
2 tomatoes, sliced

A 2 pint pie dish

Boil the leeks in salted water for 5 – 8 minutes or until they are tender, drain them well, and place in the pie dish, with the well-flavoured sauce poured on top.

Cut a quarter of the potatoes into thin slices and fry these gently in half of the butter until they are golden brown on both sides.

Cook the remaining potatoes in boiling salted water for 20 – 25 minutes until they are cooked through, then drain well and mash. Spread the mashed potato on top of the sliced potatoes and dot with the remaining butter.

Bake at 375°F (Gas Mark 5) for 25 – 30 minutes so that the surface is golden brown. Arrange the sliced tomatoes on top and return the dish to the oven for a further 5 minutes. This can be served as a light meal in itself, or as a vegetable with hot or cold meats.

Potato Scones

Serves 4

½ pound potatoes
½ ounce butter
1½ – 2 ounces self-raising flour

Cook the potatoes in boiling salted water,
drain them and mash with the butter,
seasoning with salt and pepper.

With a fork stir in the flour to form a
pliable paste. Roll out the mixture very
thinly on a floured board. Using a 3 inch
cutter, cut the potato into rounds and prick
these well.

Cook on a hot griddle or in a heavy based
frying pan for 3 minutes each side until they
are golden brown.

Serve hot with butter, or with meat and
fish dishes.

Elsie Eaton's Special Cabbage

Serves 4

½ ounce butter
1 ounce bacon, chopped
1 small onion, chopped
1 pound white cabbage, shredded
¼ pint stock
1 large cooking apple, peeled, cored and
    sliced
½ ounce plain flour
Nutmeg, freshly grated

Melt the butter in a pan and fry the bacon
and onion until it is soft. Add the shredded
cabbage and stir the ingredients together.

Pour in the stock, season well with salt
and pepper and cook for 3 minutes. Add the
apples and cook for a further 3 minutes.

Sprinkle the flour into the pan and stir
until the mixture thickens. Add a little
grated nutmeg, adjust the seasoning and
serve at once.

Baked Onions with Country Stuffing

Serves 4

2 large onions, skinned
2 tablespoons fresh white breadcrumbs
3 ounces Cheddar cheese, grated
1 tablespoon parsley, chopped
1 tablespoon tomato purée
A little stock
½ ounce butter

Cook the onions in boiling salted water for 10 – 12 minutes, and drain well. Remove the onion centres by holding the onion in a cloth and gently squeezing out the middle part.

Chop the centres finely and mix with the breadcrumbs, 2 ounces of the cheese, the parsley, tomato purée, then season with salt and pepper. Add sufficient stock to moisten the mixture.

Fill the onions with the stuffing, top each one with the remaining Cheddar cheese and dot with the butter.

Bake at 400°F (Gas Mark 6) for 25 – 30 minutes or until the onions are cooked and golden brown.

Serve as a snack or as a vegetable with tomato sauce. (see page 22)

Northumberland Pan Haggerty

Serves 4

1 ounce dripping
2 pound potatoes, cut in slices
1 pound onions, cut in slices
¼ pound Cheddar cheese, grated

Heat the dripping in a large heavy frying pan, and place in it alternate layers of potatoes and onions, separating each one with a sprinkling of cheese and seasoning.

Fry gently, covered with a lid, until the vegetables are brown.

Very Special Cauliflower Cheese

Serves 4

1 medium-sized cauliflower
1 ounce butter
1 ounce plain flour
½ pint milk
4 ounces cheese, grated
2 eggs, separated
2 tomatoes, sliced
Parsley, chopped

Cook the cauliflower in boiling salted water for 10 – 12 minutes or until it is cooked through. Allow it to cool slightly, then divide into florets.

Melt the butter in a pan, stir in the flour and cook for 2 minutes. Gradually add the milk, bring to the boil and cook for 3 minutes. Season well with salt and pepper and mix in half the cheese and the egg yolks, then allow the mixture to cool slightly. Whisk the egg whites until they are stiff and fold them into the sauce.

Place some cauliflower in an ovenproof dish, arrange half the tomatoes on top of it, and coat with half the sauce. Repeat this procedure once more, topping the dish with the remaining grated cheese.

Bake at 400°F (Gas Mark 6) for 30 minutes until the sauce has risen and turned golden brown.

Sprinkle with chopped parsley and serve at once.

Spinach Tart

Serves 4

½ pound shortcrust pastry
1 pound spinach
2 eggs, beaten
¼ pint milk
4 tablespoons double cream
1 small onion, grated
2 ounces Cheddar cheese, grated

A 7 inch flan ring and baking sheet

Roll out the pastry and line the flan ring.
Prick well and bake 'blind' at 350°F (Gas
Mark 5) for 20 – 25 minutes or until it is
cooked through but not browned.

Cook the spinach in boiling salted water
for 5 minutes, drain very well, and chop up
finely. Place this in the bottom of the tart.

Mix the eggs, milk and cream together,
season with salt and pepper and pour this
mixture over the spinach, adding the onion
and cheese as well.

Bake at 350°F (Gas Mark 5) for 30 – 35
minutes until the tart is well risen and
golden brown.

Bubble and Squeak

Serves 4 – 6

1 pound potatoes, boiled
1 pound cabbage, boiled
Nutmeg, freshly ground
2 ounces butter
½ ounce butter
2 – 3 ounces cold roast beef, sliced

Cut up the potatoes and cabbage roughly,
using left-overs if these are available, and
season well with salt, pepper and nutmeg.

Melt the 2 ounces butter in a large heavy-
based frying pan and fry the vegetables
until they are golden brown.

Melt the remaining butter in a pan and
fry the sliced beef lightly until it is heated
through. Arrange the meat in a hot serving
dish and pile the Bubble and Squeak over it.

Pease Pudding

Serves 4 – 6

½ pound split peas
1 ham bone
1 ounce butter
1 egg, beaten
A pinch of sugar
1 onion, chopped finely
1 tablespoon mixed herbs

Wash the peas and soak them overnight in
cold water. Drain well and tie loosely in a
cloth with a pinch of salt. Place this bundle
in a pan with the ham bone, cover with
boiling water and simmer for 2 – 2½ hours.

Remove the bag of peas, sieve the contents and stir in the butter, egg, sugar,
onion and mixed herbs, blending all the
ingredients together.

Place the mixture on a clean floured
cloth, tie up tightly and return to the pan
for a further ½ hour.

Untie the cloth and serve the pudding on
a hot dish with baked ham or boiled bacon.

Cakes and Biscuits

An essential part of country life has always been hospitality and entertaining. When farms and villages were separated by long distances travellers would expect – and find – food and drink offered wherever they called; so it was from necessity that the farmers' wives had a constant supply of food at their ever open doors. Because cakes and biscuits were the most convenient to offer, the greatest ingenuity was used to produce interesting varieties, and recipes were handed down by word of mouth – often rough and ready descriptions that served only to increase the variations.

Most of the pastries were rich and nourishing because the main ingredients of home-produced flour, milk, eggs and butter were freely available and freely used. Gradually these cakes and biscuits – for instance, Parkin, Eccles Cakes and Shortbread – were adopted as regional specialities, and have survived in the same form until today, when they may be purchased locally from the areas that first produced them, made in the home by you or bought in a stylised form after mass production. Recapture the flavour of these old-fashioned pastries now, with the help of the recipes in this section.

The smell of baking evokes the memories of childhood for many people, and perhaps tastes acquired in the nursery never leave us because there are few people who do not react with pleasure when they are presented with such long-time favourites as Flapjacks, Maids of Honour and Gingerbread. In the past gingerbread was shaped in decorative moulds some of which represented pictures of country life. Perhaps a new interest in cake and biscuit cooking will help to rediscover some of the forgotten traditions and equipment that were once in everyday use.

The abundance of potatoes and apples overflows into even the teatime treats of the country kitchen – Dorset Apple Cake, Cider Cake and Potato Cake will very happily accompany the more familiar Seed Cake and Rock Cakes. Make Shrewsbury Biscuits, Florentines and Scotch Pancakes too, and see how fast they disappear, along with the 'cut-and-come-again' cake, which has always been a part of every well-spread tea table, be it Dundee Cake or Farmhouse Fruitcake.

Farmhouse Fruit Cake

5 ounces butter
4 tablespoons golden syrup
2 tablespoons treacle
¼ pint milk
¼ pound dates, chopped
¼ pound currants
¼ pound sultanas
½ pound raisins, stoned
¼ pound mixed peel
½ pound self-raising flour
1 teaspoon mixed spice
1 teaspoon ground nutmeg
A pinch of cinnamon
A pinch of salt
2 eggs, beaten
½ teaspoon bicarbonate of soda

A 10 inch round cake tin, lined with greased greaseproof paper

Put the butter, syrup, treacle, milk, dried fruit and peel in a pan and heat slowly until the fat has melted. Gradually bring to the boil and simmer for 5 minutes, stirring occasionally. Allow the mixture to cool completely.

Sieve the flour, spices and salt into a bowl, and stir in the eggs. Add the bicarbonate of soda to the fruit mixture and pour this onto the flour. Beat well until all the ingredients are thoroughly mixed.

Line and grease the cake tin and pour in the mixture. Bake at 325°F (Gas Mark 3) for 1¾ hours, or until the cake is well risen and cooked through.

Scotch Sultana Cake

¼ pound butter, softened
¼ pound caster sugar
2 large eggs, beaten
½ pound self-raising flour
A pinch of salt
½ pound sultanas
Juice and grated rind of an orange
Juice and grated rind of a lemon

A 6 inch cake tin, lined with greased greaseproof paper

Mix the butter and sugar together until they are creamy, then gradually beat in the eggs until the whole mixture is light and fluffy.

Sift the flour and salt together and fold this into the creamed mixture. Add the sultanas, the rind and juice of the lemon and orange and stir well.

Turn the mixture into the cake tin and bake at 350°F (Gas Mark 4) for 1½ – 1¾ hours, or until it has risen well and is cooked through.

Cider Cake

6 ounces butter, softened
6 ounces soft brown sugar
2 eggs, beaten
½ pound self-raising flour
8 tablespoons sweet cider

A 7 inch round cake tin, lined with greased greaseproof paper

Cream the butter and sugar together until the mixture is light and fluffy. Gradually add the eggs, beating well.

Using a metal spoon, fold in the flour and cider alternately and spread the mixture into the tin.

Bake at 325°F (Gas Mark 3) for 1 hour, or until the cake has risen and is cooked through.

Gingerbread

12 ounces self-raising flour
A pinch of salt
4 teaspoons ground ginger
2 teaspoons ground cinnamon
6 ounces butter
½ pound black treacle
6 ounces soft brown sugar
2 eggs, beaten
¼ pint single cream

A 7 inch square cake tin, lined with greased greaseproof paper

Sift the flour, salt, ginger and cinnamon into a mixing bowl. Melt the butter, treacle and soft brown sugar over a low heat until it is all thoroughly dissolved.

Pour the melted ingredients onto the flour and beat with a wooden spoon. Gradually add the eggs, mixing well after each addition.

Lastly stir in the cream and pour the mixture into the prepared tin. Bake at 375°F (Gas Mark 4) for 1 hour, then reduce the temperature to 275°F (Gas Mark 1) for a further 2 hours.

Maids of Honour

¼ pound cottage cheese
3 ounces butter, softened
2 egg yolks
3 ounces caster sugar
2 tablespoons potatoes, cooked and mashed
1½ ounces ground almonds
Juice and grated rind of a lemon
Juice and grated rind of an orange
½ teaspoon almond essence
Nutmeg, freshly grated
½ pound puff pastry

Sieve the cottage cheese and mix it with the butter, beat in the egg yolks and add the sugar, mixing well.

Add the potatoes, ground almonds, rind and juice of the lemon and orange, almond essence and nutmeg.

Mix all the ingredients together and gradually add them to the cottage cheese mixture.

Use the pastry to line about 36 patty tins and fill each one three quarters full with the mixture. Bake at 400°F (Gas Mark 6) for 20 – 25 minutes until they are golden brown.

Dorset Apple Cake

½ pound self-raising flour
A pinch of cinnamon
¼ pound butter, softened
¼ pound soft brown sugar
½ pound dessert apples, coarsely chopped
    or grated
2 eggs, beaten
2 tablespoons soft brown sugar
A pinch of nutmeg, freshly grated
A pinch of cinnamon

A 9 inch cake tin lined with greased grease-proof paper

Sieve the flour and cinnamon into a bowl and rub in the butter. Add the sugar, apples and eggs then stir the mixture into a fairly stiff dough. Spread it in the prepared tin, mix the sugar and spices together and sprinkle this over the top of the cake.

Bake at 350°F (Gas Mark 5) for 30 minutes, cover with greaseproof paper and continue baking for a further 30 minutes, so that the cake has risen and cooked through.

Eccles Cakes

8 ounces flaky pastry
1 ounce butter
½ pound currants
3 ounces soft brown sugar
1 ounce mixed peel
A pinch of mixed spice
A pinch of cinnamon
1 egg white, beaten
Caster sugar

Roll out the pastry to just under ¼ inch thick. Cut into rounds between 2½ and 3½ inches in diameter, using a large scone cutter or a small cup.

Place the butter, currants, sugar, mixed peel and spices in a bowl and mix together. Place a little of this filling in the centre of each pastry round.

Brush the edge with beaten egg white, and gather the pastry to the centre pressing it together. Turn each cake over so that the join is underneath.

Make two small cuts on top of the Eccles Cakes and brush with beaten egg white. Sprinkle with caster sugar and bake at 425°F (Gas Mark 7) for 10 – 12 minutes, so that the cakes are golden brown.

Dundee Cake

6 ounces butter, softened
6 ounces soft brown sugar
½ pound self-raising flour
A pinch of salt
1 teaspoon ground nutmeg
1 teaspoon mixed spice
3 large eggs, beaten
1 pound mixed dried fruit
2 ounces split almonds

A 7 inch round cake tin, lined with greased greaseproof paper

Cream the butter and sugar together until the mixture is light and fluffy. Sieve the flour, salt and spices together and put them on one side.

Gradually beat the eggs into the butter and sugar until they are thoroughly mixed, then carefully fold in the flour mixture and stir in the dried fruit.

Put it all into the prepared tin, and arrange the almonds in an attractive pattern on top.

Bake at 350°F (Gas Mark 4) for 1 hour, then reduce the temperature to 300°F (Gas Mark 2) for a further 1¼ hours.

Scotch Pancakes

Makes approximately 25 – 30 pancakes

2 ounces butter
1 teaspoon golden syrup
5 ounces plain flour
A pinch of salt
1 level teaspoon bicarbonate of soda
1 level teaspoon cream of tartar
1 teaspoon caster sugar
1 egg, beaten
1 level teaspoon baking powder
A small quantity of milk

A griddle or heavy-based frying pan, greased

Melt the butter and syrup together in a pan. Sift the flour, salt, bicarbonate of soda and cream of tartar into a mixing bowl, add the sugar and beat in the egg. Lastly stir in the baking powder and mix well together to form a thick batter, adding extra milk if necessary to give it the consistency of thick cream.

Using a tablespoon, drop the mixture onto a hot griddle and cook for 2 – 3 minutes so that bubbles form and burst on the surface. Carefully turn each pancake over, using a palette knife, and cook the other side.

Cool on a wire rack and serve spread with butter.

Grandma's Parkin

¼ pound self-raising flour
4 teaspoons ground ginger
A pinch of salt
½ pound medium oatmeal
2 ounces butter
¼ pound golden syrup
¼ pound black treacle
¼ pound soft brown sugar
1 large egg, beaten
A small quantity of milk

A 7 inch square cake tin lined with greased greaseproof paper

Sift the flour, ginger and salt into a bowl and stir in the oatmeal, mixing the ingredients together thoroughly.

Melt the butter, syrup, treacle and soft brown sugar over a low heat, and pour this into the dry ingredients, stirring well.

Gradually add the beaten egg and add sufficient milk to make a soft dropping consistency.

Turn into the prepared tin and bake at 325°F (Gas Mark 3) for about 1 hour, or until the Parkin is golden brown.

Cool on a wire rack and store in an airtight tin.

Treacle Scones

Makes 18 – 20 scones

1 pound wholemeal flour
2 teaspoons bicarbonate of soda
4 teaspoons cream of tarter
A pinch of salt
1 teaspoon ground ginger
1 teaspoon ground cinnamon
3 ounces butter
2 ounces soft brown sugar
2 level tablespoons black treacle
¼ pint milk

A plain round 2 inch cutter
1 – 2 baking sheets, greased

Place the wholemeal flour in a mixing bowl and sift in the bicarbonate of soda, cream of tartar, salt, ground ginger and cinnamon. Mix all this together, and rub in the butter so that the mixture resembles fine breadcrumbs, then add the sugar.

Blend the treacle and milk together, and stir this into the dry ingredients. Mix to a soft dough adding more milk if necessary.

Roll out the dough on a floured pastry board to about ¾ inch and cut into rounds. Place them on the prepared baking sheets.

Bake at 425°F (Gas Mark 7) for 10 minutes, or until they are golden brown. Cool the scones between the folds of a tea towel to keep the surface soft.

Serve with butter.

Shortbread

5 ounces plain flour
1 ounce rice flour
2 ounces caster sugar
4 ounces butter
Caster sugar

1 baking sheet, greased
A wooden shortbread mould or 7 inch
sandwich tin

Sift the flours and add the sugar. Gradually work in the butter to form a firm dough. Knead well and press firmly into the shortbread mould or sandwich tin.

Refrigerate or chill for 30 minutes. Carefully turn out the shortbread onto the prepared baking sheet, prick well and mark into cutting sections.

Bake at 325°F (Gas Mark 3) for 45 minutes until it is golden brown.

Dredge with caster sugar, cut into sections and store in an airtight tin.

Shrewsbury Biscuits

¼ pound butter
¼ pound caster sugar
1 small egg, beaten
2 teaspoons grated lemon rind
½ pound plain flour
A pinch of cinnamon

2 baking sheets, greased
1 inch pastry cutter

Cream the butter and sugar together until the mixture is light and fluffy, then beat in the egg and mix thoroughly.

Stir in the lemon rind, and gradually fold in the sifted flour and cinnamon.

Knead the mixture lightly and place it on a floured pastry board. Roll out thinly, prick well all over and cut into rounds, using a 1 inch cutter.

Place on the prepared baking sheets and bake at 350°F (Gas Mark 4) for 15 minutes.

Cool on a wire rack and store in an airtight tin.

Seed Cake

6 ounces butter
6 ounces caster sugar
3 large eggs
Juice and grated rind of an orange
½ pound self-raising flour
1 tablespoon caraway seeds

A 7 inch cake tin, lined with greased
greaseproof paper

Cream the butter and sugar in a bowl until the mixture is light and fluffy. Gradually beat in the eggs until they are thoroughly mixed, and add the orange juice and rind.

Sift the flour and fold this into the mixture. Lastly stir in the caraway seeds.

Turn into the prepared cake tin and bake at 350°F (Gas Mark 4) for 1¼ – 1½ hours until the cake has risen well and cooked through.

Potato Cake

¼ pound shredded suet or butter
¾ pound self-raising flour
¼ pound caster sugar
¼ pound raisins
6 ounces hot potatoes, mashed
1 large egg, beaten
A small quantity of milk

A 7 inch cake tin, well greased

Rub the fat into the flour until it resembles
fine breadcrumbs, and stir in the sugar
and raisins.

Add the potato and mix well, then use the
egg to bind the mixture together, adding a
little milk if the consistency is too stiff.

Turn into the prepared cake tin and bake
at 350°F (Gas Mark 4) for about 1 hour, or
until golden brown.

Serve hot with plenty of butter.

Spiced Coffee Drops

½ pound butter
1 pound soft brown sugar
2 large eggs, beaten
¼ pint cold strong coffee
1 pound plain flour
1 level teaspoon bicarbonate of soda
A pinch of salt
1 level teaspoon ground nutmeg
1 level teaspoon cinnamon
1 level teaspoon mixed spice

2 baking sheets, greased

Cream together the butter and sugar until
the mixture is light and fluffy. Gradually
beat in the eggs until they are thoroughly
mixed, then add the coffee.

Sift the flour, soda, salt and spices
together and fold these dry ingredients
into the mixture, which can then be shaped
into balls.

Refrigerate or stand them in a cool place
for 30 – 40 minutes until they are firm.

Bake at 400°F (Gas Mark 6) for 10 – 12
minutes, and cool on a wire tray. Store in
an airtight tin.

Grantham Gingerbreads

¼ pound butter
¼ pound caster sugar
¼ pound self raising flour
2 teaspoons ground ginger

2 baking sheets, ungreased

Cream the butter and sugar together until
they are light and fluffy.

Sift the flour and ginger together and
gradually stir this into the creamed
mixture to make a firm dough.

Roll this into balls and place them on
the baking sheets. Flatten the biscuits
slightly and bake at 200°F (Gas Mark ½) for
45 minutes until the outside of each one is
crisp and the middle is soft.

Allow to cool on a wire rack and store
in an airtight tin.

Flapjacks

6 ounces butter
¼ pound demerara sugar
2 tablespoons golden syrup
Vanilla essence
½ pound porridge oats

An 11 x 7 inch swiss roll tin, greased

Warm the butter, sugar and syrup in a
pan, and dissolve the ingredients
completely before stirring in the vanilla
essence and porridge oats.

Spread the mixture evenly in the tin and
bake at 375°F (Gas Mark 5) for 15 – 20
minutes until the biscuit is golden brown
and firm.

Cut into fingers or squares and cool on a
wire rack. Store in an airtight tin.

Florentines

¼ pound caster sugar
¼ pound butter
4 tablespoons golden syrup
3 ounces glacé cherries, chopped
2 ounces blanched almonds, chopped
2 ounces walnuts, chopped
¼ pound self-raising flour
A pinch of salt
½ pound plain chocolate

*2 baking sheets lined with greased
greaseproof paper or vegetable parchment*

Gently dissolve the sugar, butter and
golden syrup in a pan. Stir in the cherries
and nuts and allow to cool slightly, then
stir in the flour and salt and cool
completely.

Place teaspoonfuls of the mixture on the
prepared baking sheets, making sure that
each Florentine has plenty of room for
spreading.

Bake at 350°F (Gas Mark 4) for 10 – 12
minutes until they are a deep golden
brown. Allow them to cool slightly before
moving to a wire rack.

Cut the chocolate into small pieces,
place it in a bowl over hot water and allow
to melt. Using a palette knife, spread the
underside of the Florentines with the
chocolate and draw a fork over the
surface to produce a wavy pattern. Allow
the chocolate to set, then store the biscuits
in an airtight tin.

Rock Cakes

Makes 17 – 18 rock cakes

½ pound self-raising flour
1 teaspoon nutmeg, freshly grated
¼ pound granulated sugar
¼ pound butter
2 ounces sultanas
1 egg, beaten

2 baking sheets, greased

Sift the flour and nutmeg into a mixing
bowl and add the sugar. Rub the butter
into the mixture until it resembles fine
breadcrumbs, then stir in the sultanas and
the egg.

Form the mixture into rough balls and
place on the baking sheets. Bake at 350°F
(Gas Mark 4) for 20 minutes until the cakes
are golden brown.

Cool on a wire rack and store in an
airtight tin.

Coventry God Cakes

½ pound puff pastry
¼ – ½ pound home-made mincemeat
1 egg white, beaten
Caster sugar

Roll out the pastry to ¼ inch thick and cut
into 4 inch squares. Place a good
teaspoonful of mincemeat on the centre of
each one.

Dampen the edges with egg white, draw
up the corners to the centre of the cake and
press together firmly.

Brush the cakes with egg white and
sprinkle with caster sugar. Bake at 425°F
(Gas Mark 7) for 10 – 15 minutes until they
are well risen and golden brown.

A mystique surrounds the making of bread, and for those whose knowledge of this staff of life extends only to a large sliced white loaf, it will probably be surprising to learn how easy it is to make your own bread. An increasing interest in wholesome natural food, with a growing suspicion of the chemical additives in commercially produced bread has led many people to make their own. Bread plays a major part in the diet of many households therefore it is obviously one of the best things to make at home.

Coarse-ground flour that has undergone far fewer processes than finely milled white flour makes a nourishing bread with an interesting taste and texture. Because bread was eaten in such quantities by country families, cooks were keen to vary the taste as much as possible. Because of this they created a huge range of loaves which varied in size, shape, texture and flavour. We have become so accustomed to large square sliced loaves, it is no wonder that an old-fashioned baker's shop, filled with a rich assortment of long and short sticks of bread, poppy seed buns, cottage loaves and little crispy rolls, makes our mouths water and reveals to us that bread is a food to enjoy and savour.

Because of the close association of the land with grain, flour and bread, the most basic of country customs, many with their roots in pagan times, are connected with wheat, barley and oats. Legends surrounding them, such as the one about corn dollies

which are sacrificed to restore fertility to the crops for the coming year, make fascinating reading for anyone really intrigued by the customs of the countryside.

The housewife who makes her own bread is reflecting the image held in many peoples' minds of what represents a real home – the warm kitchen, the yeasty smell of dough rising in a bowl on the stove and the marvellous aroma of baking loaves. Surely it is worth the small effort involved to follow the recipes in this section, and so give your family homemade bread, and also loaves and buns that have traditional country origins, for example Spiced Apple Tea Bread, Irish Soda Bread and Wiltshire Lardy Cakes.

Chelsea Buns

Makes 16 buns

½ ounce fresh yeast, or 1 teaspoon dried
yeast
Just over ¼ pint milk, warmed to blood
heat
1 pound strong flour
A pinch of salt
2 ounces caster sugar
2 ounces butter
2 eggs, beaten
Filling:
1 ounce butter
2 ounces soft brown sugar
1 teaspoon mixed spice
A pinch of nutmeg
4 ounces currants

Two 7 inch sandwich tins, greased

Place the yeast in a basin and mix in the
milk.

Sift the flour and salt into a bowl, add
the sugar and rub in the butter until
the mixture resembles fine breadcrumbs.

Gradually add the milk and yeast,
beating well. Knead the dough thoroughly
and place it in an oiled polythene bag in a
warm place until it has doubled in size
which takes about 20 – 30 minutes.

Knead the dough again and roll it out to
a square about 18 x 18 inches on a floured
board.

Melt the butter and brush it over the
dough. Sprinkle with brown sugar, the
spices and currants. Roll up the dough and
cut the length into sixteen pieces.

Arrange the circular buns in the
prepared tins, and put these in polythene
bags in a warm place, until the dough has
doubled in size.

Bake at 375°F (Gas Mark 5) for 30
minutes until the buns are golden brown.
Serve with butter.

Irish Soda Bread

½ pound plain flour
1 tablespoon baking powder
1 teaspoon bicarbonate of soda
A pinch of salt
1½ pounds wholemeal flour
1 tablespoon caster sugar
1 ounce butter
¾ pint warm milk

1 baking sheet, greased

Sift the plain flour, baking powder,
bicarbonate of soda and salt into a bowl
and mix in the wholemeal flour.

Add the sugar and rub the butter into the
dry ingredients so that the mixture
resembles fine breadcrumbs. Mix to a stiff
dough with the warm milk, and knead until
it is smooth.

Shape it into an oblong loaf, score across
the top and bake at 400°F (Gas Mark 6)
for 1 hour until the loaf has risen and
turned golden brown.

Sally Lunn

2 ounces butter
¼ pint of milk
1 teaspoon caster sugar
½ ounce fresh yeast (or 2 level teaspoons
dried yeast)
2 eggs, beaten
1 pound strong plain flour
1 level teaspoon salt

Two 5 inch round cake tins

Melt the butter in a pan then remove from
the heat and add the milk and sugar. Blend
the yeast and milk mixture together and
stir in the beaten eggs.

Sift the flour and salt into a bowl, add
the yeast mixture and knead well. Divide
the mixture in half and put into the lightly
greased tins. Allow the dough to rise in a
warm place until it doubles in size, about
1 hour.

Bake at 450° (Gas Mark 8) for 15-20
minutes. Turn out onto a wire rack to cool.

Cut the teacakes in half, spread with
butter, and sandwich together before
serving.

Singing Hinnies

1 pound plain flour
A pinch of salt
A pinch of cream of tartar
A pinch of bicarbonate of soda
¼ pound lard
¼ pound butter
3 ounces currants
A small quantity of milk

A griddle or heavy-based frying pan

Sift the flour, salt, cream of tartar and
bicarbonate of soda into a bowl, and rub
the lard and butter into the mixture until
it resembles fine breadcrumbs.

Add the currants, stir well and add
sufficient milk to make a firm dough. Shape
the dough into a round and roll it out to
¼ inch thick.

Grease a griddle or heavy-based frying
pan and place the cake on it.

Cook for 10 minutes until the scone is
golden brown then turn it over and cook
the other side.

Divide into sections and serve hot with
butter.

Wiltshire Lardy Cake

½ pound strong flour
A pinch of salt
A pinch of mixed spice
½ ounce fresh yeast, or 2 teaspoons dried
  yeast
1 teaspoon sugar
¼ pink milk, warmed to blood heat
2 ounces lard
2 ounces sugar
2 ounces dried fruit
1 egg, beaten

Sift the flour, salt and spice together
into a bowl.

Cream the yeast and sugar together,
add this to the dry ingredients and mix
together with sufficient milk to make a
soft dough then knead well.

Cover the bowl and stand it aside until
the dough has doubled in size. Roll out on a
floured board to ¼ inch thick.

Spread on half the lard, sugar and fruit.
Fold in three, turn the dough to the left
and roll out again.

Cover with the rest of the lard, sugar
and fruit, and fold in three again.

Roll out to an oblong 1 inch thick. Place
in a deep tin and stand in a warm place
until it is well risen. Score the top with a
knife.

Brush with beaten egg and bake at
425°F (Gas Mark 7) for 25 – 30 minutes
until golden brown. Cool on a wire rack.

Yorkshire Teacakes

Makes 6

1 ounce fresh yeast or ½ ounce dried yeast
1 ascorbic acid tablet
½ pint warm milk, warmed to blood heat
1 pound strong flour
1 level teaspoon salt
1 ounce caster sugar
1 ounce butter
4 ounces mixed dried fruit
1 egg, beaten

2 baking sheets, greased

Place the yeast in a small bowl with the ascorbic acid tablet. Pour in the warm milk and blend until the tablet has dissolved.

Sift the flour and salt into a mixing bowl, add the sugar and rub in the butter until the mixture resembles fine breadcrumbs.

Add the fruit and mix in the yeast liquid to form a firm dough.

Turn this onto a floured pastry board and knead thoroughly until it is smooth and elastic which takes about 10 minutes.

Form the dough into 6 equal pieces, knead each one and roll out to 4 inches across.

Place well apart on the prepared baking sheets, cover with a piece of oiled polythene and leave in a warm place so the dough doubles its size.

Brush the surface with beaten egg and bake at 400°F (Gas Mark 6) for 20 minutes until the teacakes are golden brown.

Serve hot or toasted with butter.

Spiced Apple Teabread

2 ounces butter
¾ pound self-raising flour
A pinch of salt
A pinch of allspice
A pinch of ground nutmeg
1 teaspoon mixed spice
3 ounces soft brown sugar
2 large eggs
6 tablespoons single cream
10 ounces Bramley apples, grated
3 ounces dates, stoned and chopped
½ ounce walnuts, chopped

A 2 pound loaf tin, greased

Melt the butter in a pan. Sift the flour, salt and spices into a mixing bowl and add the brown sugar.

Beat the eggs in a basin, blend in the melted butter and cream and stir this liquid into the dry ingredients. Add the apples, dates and walnuts, mixing well.

Turn the mixture into the prepared tin and bake at 325°F (Gas Mark 3) for 1½ hours until it is golden brown.

Cool on a wire rack and store in an airtight tin. Serve sliced and spread with butter.

White or Wholemeal Bread

3 pounds strong flour or wholemeal flour
1 ounce salt
1 ounce butter
1 ounce fresh yeast or $\frac{1}{2}$ ounce dried yeast
1 teaspoon caster sugar
Approximately 1$\frac{1}{2}$ pints tepid water

Two 2 pound loaf tins, or four 1 pound loaf tins

Sift the flour and salt into a bowl, and rub the fat into the dry ingredients until it resembles fine breadcrumbs.

Place the yeast in a basin, add the sugar and some tepid water. Cover and leave until it turns frothy in about 10 – 15 minutes.

Add the creamed yeast to the flour mixture and mix well together. Knead the dough on a floured board thoroughly for about 10 minutes.

Place the dough in a greased bowl, cover with a large oiled polythene bag and stand in a warm place for 45 – 50 minutes until it has doubled in size.

Turn the dough onto a floured board and knead well for about 5 minutes.

Grease the loaf tins and divide the mixture into half or quarters to fit the appropriate tins.

Place the tins in a warm place to double in size and then bake at 400°F (Gas Mark 6) for 40 minutes for 1 pound loaves and 1 hour for 2 pound loaves.

Cool on wire racks and store in a breadbin.

Gipsy Malt Loaf

$\frac{1}{2}$ pound plain flour
A pinch of salt
1 level teaspoon bicarbonate of soda
2 ounces golden syrup
1 ounce soft brown sugar
2 tablespoons malt
2 ounces raisins
2 ounces sultanas
1 ounce dates, chopped
$\frac{1}{4}$ pint milk, approximately

A 1 pound loaf tin, lined with greased greaseproof paper

Sift the flour, salt and bicarbonate of soda into a mixing bowl.

Gently melt the syrup, sugar and malt in a pan and pour it onto the dry ingredients. Mix well, add the dried fruit and mix to a stiff consistency with the milk.

Turn into the prepared loaf tin and bake at 350°F (Gas Mark 3) for 1 – 1$\frac{1}{4}$ hours until the loaf has risen and turned golden brown.

Cool on a wire rack and store in an airtight tin for at least 2 days before eating, then serve it sliced and buttered.

Yorkshire Bun Loaf

10 ounces self-raising flour
A pinch of salt
¼ pound butter
3 ounces caster sugar
2 large eggs, beaten
1 tablespoon marmalade
3 ounces sultanas
3 ounces currants
A small quantity of milk
Caster sugar

A 2 pound loaf tin, greased

Sift the flour and salt into a mixing bowl. Rub in the butter until the mixture resembles fine breadcrumbs.

Add sugar and gradually mix in the eggs, then the marmalade and dried fruit, using sufficient milk to make a fairly stiff mixture. Turn it into the prepared tin, and sprinkle the top with caster sugar.

Bake at 375°F (Gas Mark 5) for 1 hour or until it has risen and turned golden brown.

Allow to cool on a wire rack and store in an airtight tin. Serve sliced and buttered.

Spiced Fruit Loaf

1 pound plain flour
1 teaspoon grated nutmeg
1 teaspoon mixed spice
3 ounces lard
3 ounces butter
6 ounces soft brown sugar
2 ounces mixed peel
¼ pound mixed dried fruit
1 tablespoon golden syrup
½ pint milk
1 teaspoon bicarbonate of soda
1 tablespoon malt vinegar

A 2 pound loaf tin, greased

Sift the flour and spices into a mixing bowl. Rub the lard and butter into the dry ingredients until the mixture resembles fine breadcrumbs.

Add the sugar, peel and fruit and stir in the syrup and milk.

Mix the bicarbonate of soda and vinegar together and quickly add this to the mixture. Stir thoroughly and turn it into the prepared tin.

Bake at 350°F (Gas Mark 4) for 2 hours until the loaf is golden brown. Cool for 15 minutes in the tin and then transfer to a wire rack. Store in an airtight tin and serve sliced with butter.

Puddings and Desserts

If there is one field of cooking in which the British cooks excel it must be in their huge and varied range of delicious puddings and desserts. Light suet puddings, hot sweet roly-polys, pies and tarts, crumbles and rich milk puddings, all are familiar and much-appreciated conclusions to a traditional meal.

When you see the enormous variety of dishes in this section, you will have to try them—choose from Rice Pudding, Bread and Butter Pudding, Egg Custard and Queen of Puddings. The puddings are high in nutritive value because they make use of fresh eggs, milk and cream.

The sweet course allows country cooks to serve some of the plentiful supply of fresh fruit. However, we can all preserve fresh produce, or use fruit that has been frozen, bottled, canned or dried for use out of season so we are no longer limited to making a particular pudding only at one time of the year. As much a part of summer as its name suggests is Summer Pudding, renowned as a special delight, and although like many recipes it specifies raspberries, currants and blackberries, it is possible to use one or a combination of many soft fruits, depending on what is available. Alternatively, add preserved fruit to fresh fruit to make for greater variety. Some fruit is free too since all over the countryside in the autumn you can pick blackberries from the hedgerows and woods; and the achievement of gathering

them in a basket is equalled only by the pleasure of cooking and eating a Blackberry and Apple Crumble.

The dessert course may be an extravagant and decorative one, and it should not be imagined that country fare is always plain. Charlotte Russe and Suffolk Fruit Trifle, even fresh Strawberries and Cream make an excellent end to any meal, whilst Old English Syllabub, by its name alone, echoes the best of extravagant festive cooking. The Nottingham Pancake Layer proves that it is not necessary to wait for Shrove Tuesday, for pancakes are so full of goodness that they may be served at any time of the year. However the significance of the festival is never forgotten by country housewives who honour the tradition of finishing up all the eggs, milk and flour in the house before the Lenten fast begins.

Rich Cabinet Pudding

Serves 4 – 6

2 ounces glacé cherries, halved
Strips of angelica
¾ pint milk
2 large eggs
2 tablespoons caster sugar
A few drops of vanilla essence
3 small sponge cakes
1 ounce ratafia biscuits

A 5 inch round cake tin

Line the bottom of the cake tin with greased greaseproof paper. Decorate with a few cherries and angelica leaves.

Warm the milk, and whisk the eggs and sugar together, flavouring with the vanilla essence, then stir this into the milk.

Crumble the sponge cakes and ratafia biscuits and put them in the tin with the remaining cherries.

Strain the milk mixture over the cakes and allow them to soak for ¼ hour. Cover the tin with greaseproof paper and steam over boiling water for about 1 hour until the pudding is firm

Turn it out onto a dish and serve with custard.

Banbury Apple Pie

Serves 4 – 6

½ pound shortcrust pastry
1 pound cooking apples, peeled, cored and sliced
2 ounces cut mixed peel
A pinch of nutmeg
Soft brown sugar
1 tablespoon milk
Caster sugar

An 8 inch pie plate

Divide the pastry in two and use half to line the pie plate.

Place the prepared apples, peel and nutmeg in a basin with sugar according to taste. Mix all the ingredients together and put the fruit into the pie plate.

Roll out the remaining pastry and lift it over the rolling pin onto the apples. Seal and flute the edges and make a small hole in the centre of the pie to allow the steam to escape

Brush with the milk and bake at 400°F (Gas Mark 6) for 35 – 40 minutes until the pie is golden brown. Dredge with caster sugar and serve hot or cold with cream or custard.

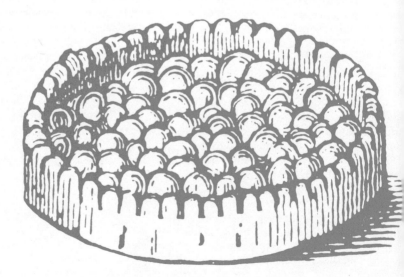

Bakewell Tart

Serves 4 – 6

6 ounces puff pastry
2 tablespoons strawberry jam
2 ounces butter
2 ounces caster sugar
Juice and grated rind of ½ lemon
1 large egg, beaten
3 ounces self-raising flour
3 ounces ground almonds

A 7 or 8 inch pie plate

Roll out the pastry and line the pie plate.
Spread the jam over the base of the pastry.

Cream the butter and sugar together
until the mixture is light and fluffy, then
add the lemon rind and juice and gradually
beat in the egg.

Sift the flour and fold it into the mixture
with the ground almonds. Put the almond
pastry into the pie plate and smooth it with
a knife.

Bake at 425°F (Gas Mark 7) for 15
minutes, and then reduce the temperature
to 350°F (Gas Mark 4) for a further 20 – 30
minutes, so that the tart is firm to the
touch.

Serve hot or cold with cream or custard.

Mincemeat Apples

Serves 4

4 large even-sized Bramley apples,
    with the cores removed
¾ pound mincemeat
Juice and grated rind of a lemon
2 tablespoons demerara sugar
4 tablespoons water

Cut each apple in half horizontally and fill
the centres with mincemeat. Replace the
halves together, and spoon a little extra
mincemeat onto the top of each apple.

Sprinkle them with the lemon juice, rind
and sugar, then place the apples in an
ovenproof dish surrounded by the water.

Bake at 375°F (Gas Mark 5) for 40 – 45
minutes. Serve either hot or cold.

Charlotte Russe

Serves 6

20 sponge fingers
1 pint double cream
½ pound caster sugar
Juice of 3 lemons
1 ounce gelatine dissolved in
    1 tablespoon of water
4 tablespoons brandy
2 eggs, separated
Decoration:
¼ pint double cream, whipped
Candied violets and angelica
A piece of ribbon

An 8 inch loose-bottomed cake tin
A piping bag and star nozzle

Trim the rounded part off one end of each
biscuit so that they will stand upright
round the edge of the tin with the sugared
part towards the outside.

Whip the double cream until it is fairly
stiff.

Dissolve the sugar and lemon juice in a
pan, add the gelatine and brandy and beat
in the yolks. Allow to cool but not to set.

Whisk the egg whites until they are very
stiff. Gradually beat the gelatine mixture
into the cream and fold in egg whites. Pour
this mixture into the prepared cake tin and
refrigerate until it is set.

Turn out carefully onto a flat serving
dish, and tie the piece of ribbon round the
middle of the biscuits. Pipe the cream in
rosettes along the edge of the Charlotte
Russe and decorate with candied violets
and angelica leaves.

Strawberries and Cream

Serves 4

1 pound fresh strawberries
Juice and grated rind of an orange
2 tablespoons caster sugar
2 tablespoons brandy
¼ pint double cream

Hull the strawberries and place them in a
bowl. Put the rind and strained juice of the
orange in a basin with the sugar and
brandy, stirring well until the sugar has
dissolved.

Whip the cream until it just holds its
shape then fold it into the orange mixture

Pour the cream over the strawberries,
cover and chill for at least half an hour.
Serve with shortbread fingers.

Blackberry and Apple Crumble

Serves 4 – 6

1 pound Bramley cooking apples, peeled,
   cored and sliced
½ pound blackberries
2 tablespoons water
Sugar
6 ounces plain flour
3 ounces caster sugar
3 ounces butter

Place the apples in a pan with the cleaned
blackberries, add the water and stew the
fruit until it is soft. Stir in sugar according
to taste.

Sift the flour into a bowl, add the sugar
and rub in the butter until the mixture
resembles fine breadcrumbs.

Put the blackberries and apple in an
ovenproof dish and sprinkle the crumble
over the top.

Bake at 400°F (Gas Mark 6) for 20 – 30
minutes. Serve hot with cream or custard.

Farmhouse Roly Poly

Serves 4

6 ounces suetcrust pastry
4 – 6 tablespoons damson jam or other type
   of home-made jam or mincemeat
A small quantity of milk

*Aluminium foil – 9 by 12 inches in size,
and lightly greased*
A steamer

Roll the pastry out on a floured pastry
board to a shape approximately 8 by 10
inches.

Spread the jam or mincemeat over the
pastry, leaving ¼ inch clear round the
outside.

Brush the edges with milk and roll up
the pastry evenly.

Place the roly poly on the foil and brush
it with a little milk. Wrap it up loosely,
allowing room for it to rise, and seal the
edges of the foil thoroughly.

Cook in a steamer for 1½ – 2 hours.
Remove from the foil and serve hot with
custard.

Gooseberry Fool

Serves 4

1 pound fresh gooseberries (or 1 pound
   4 ounce can, drained)
2 ounces sugar
¼ pint custard
¼ pint double cream
Green colouring – optional
Walnuts, chopped

Top and tail the gooseberries and stew in
a little water and sugar (unless the canned
fruit is used). Press the fruit through a
sieve, or blend it in a liquidiser.

Mix the fruit purée and custard
together, whip the cream and stir it in as
well. Add a few drops of green colouring if
the mixture is too pale.

Pour into four individual glasses and
decorate with the walnuts. Chill and serve
with shortbread fingers or plain sweet
biscuits.

Apple Dumplings

Serves 4

$\frac{1}{2}$ pound shortcrust pastry
4 even-sized Bramley cooking apples,
    peeled and cored
2 ounces demerara sugar
2 ounces sultanas
1 teaspoon cinnamon
A small quantity of milk
Caster sugar

1 baking sheet, greased

Divide the pastry into four and roll out
each piece into a circle 8 by 10 inches.

Place an apple on each pastry round and
fill the centres with sugar, sultanas and
cinnamon.

Moisten the edges of the pastry with
water, gather the edges to the tops, pressing well to seal them together. Turn the
dumplings over so that the join is
underneath.

Place the apple dumplings on the baking
sheet and brush them well with milk.

Bake at 425°F (Gas Mark 7) for 15
minutes, and reduce temperature to 325°F
(Gas Mark 3) for a further 25 – 30 minutes
so that the pastry is golden brown and the
apples are soft. Dredge with caster sugar
and serve hot or cold with custard or cream.

Westmorland Cheesecake

Serves 4 – 6

6 ounces shortcrust pastry
1$\frac{1}{2}$ ounces sultanas
Juice and grated rind of a lemon
$\frac{1}{2}$ pound cottage cheese
2 tablespoons double cream
2 tablespoons honey
2 eggs, separated
1 teaspoon cinnamon
4 ounces walnuts, chopped

An 8 inch flan ring

Use the pastry to line the flan ring, and
sprinkle the sultanas and lemon rind over
the base.

Blend the cottage cheese, cream, honey,
lemon juice and egg yolks together, then
whisk the egg whites stiffly and carefully
fold them into the cheese mixture.

Pour it all into the pastry case, flatten
with a knife and sprinkle with cinnamon.

Bake at 425°F (Gas Mark 7) for 15
minutes, then reduce the temperature to
375°F (Gas Mark 5) and bake for a further
30 minutes. Sprinkle liberally with the
chopped walnuts and serve chilled.

Taunton Treacle Tart

Serves 4 – 6

½ pound shortcrust pastry
6 tablespoons golden syrup
1 tablespoon black treacle
Juice and grated rind of ½ lemon
A pinch of ground nutmeg
5 tablespoons fresh white breadcrumbs
1 tablespoon double cream

An 8 inch pie plate

Roll out the pastry and line the pie plate
in the usual way.

Warm the syrup, treacle, rind and juice
of the lemon over a low heat and stir in the
nutmeg. Remove from the stove, stir in the
breadcrumbs, cool slightly and add the
cream.

Pour the syrup mixture into the pastry
case and bake at 425°F (Gas Mark 7) for 20
minutes so that the pastry is golden brown.
Serve warm or cold with cream or custard.

Rhubarb Charlotte

Serves 4 – 6

¼ pound fresh white breadcrumbs
3 ounces demerara sugar
3 ounces shredded suet
Grated rind of a lemon
1 teaspoon ground ginger
1½ pounds rhubarb, trimmed, washed and
   cut into short lengths
½ ounce butter

A 2 pint pie dish, greased

Place the breadcrumbs in a bowl and stir in
the sugar, suet, lemon rind and ground
ginger until everything is thoroughly
mixed together.

Put half the rhubarb in the dish, cover it
with half the crumb mixture, add the remaining fruit and top it with the rest of the
crumble.

Dot with butter and bake at 350°F (Gas
Mark 4) for 45 minutes until the fruit is
soft and the top is crisp and brown.

Bread and Butter Pudding

Serves 4 – 6

4 ounces butter, softened
12 slices white bread, thinly cut from
   a small loaf
3 ounces currants
2 ounces sultanas or raisins
1 ounce chopped mixed peel
1 ounce demerara sugar
2 large eggs
1 pint milk
2 ounces caster sugar
Vanilla essence

A 2 pint pie dish, buttered

Spread the butter fairly thickly and evenly
over the bread, cutting the slices in half
diagonally. Put a layer of bread and butter
in the base of the dish.

Mix the dried fruit and demerara sugar
together and sprinkle some of this over the
bread, then continue with alternate layers.
finishing off with bread and butter.

Beat the eggs well, stir in the milk,
sugar and a few drops of vanilla essence.
Pour this mixture over the bread.

Bake at 350°F (Gas Mark 4) for 40
minutes so that the pudding is golden
brown and cooked through.

An Especially Good Rice Pudding

Serves 4 – 6

2 ounces pudding rice
1 ounce demerara sugar
A pinch of salt
1 large can evaporated milk, made up to
   1½ pints with water
Knob of butter

A 1½ pint pie dish, greased

Wash and drain the rice and place in the
pie dish. Sprinkle in the sugar and salt,
pour the diluted evaporated milk over
the rice and mix well.

Dot with the butter and bake at 300°F
(Gas Mark 2) for 3 - 4 hours until the
surface is golden brown. Serve hot or cold.

Suffolk Fruit Trifle

Serves 6

1 pound fresh strawberries
½ pound green grapes
5 ounces macaroons
3 egg whites
5 ounces caster sugar
½ pint double cream
¼ pint dry white wine
Juice of ½ lemon
2 tablespoons brandy

Hull the strawberries and arrange with the grapes alternately round the base of a glass dish, reserving a few of the strawberries for decoration.

Break up the macaroons and sprinkle a layer on top of the fruit then continue layering, finishing with fruit.

Place the egg whites in a mixing bowl and whisk until they are very stiff. Add half the sugar, whisk again and then fold in the remaining sugar.

Whip the cream until it just holds its shape and stir in the wine, lemon juice and brandy.

Carefully fold the egg whites into the cream and pour this over the fruit. Chill for a couple of hours.

Decorate with the remaining strawberries and serve at once.

Queen of Puddings

Serves 4 – 6

1 pint milk
Rind of a lemon, thinly sliced
1 ounce caster sugar
6 ounces fresh white breadcrumbs
2 ounces butter
2 eggs, separated
2 ounces caster sugar
3 tablespoons strawberry jam

A 1½ – 2 pint pie dish, greased
A piping bag and star shaped nozzle –
optional

Pour the milk into a pan, add the lemon rind, bring to the boil and remove from the heat.

Put the sugar, breadcrumbs and butter in a bowl. Strain in the milk and beat very well adding the egg yolks and mixing well.

Pour this into the pie dish and bake at 350°F (Gas Mark 4) for 30 minutes.

Whip the egg whites until they are very stiff, and gradually whisk in the caster sugar, continuing until stiff peaks are formed.

Spread the strawberry jam over the top of the pudding and pipe or pile the meringue on top.

Continue baking for a further 15 minutes to brown the meringue. Serve hot.

Summer Pudding

Serves 4 – 6

2 tablespoons water
5 ounces sugar
½ pound blackcurrants
¼ pound blackberries
¼ pound raspberries
4 – 6 ounces white bread, cut in
   thin slices

A 1½ pint pudding basin

Stir the water and sugar together in a pan
and bring slowly to the boil.

Wash and prepare the fruit and add to the
pan, stewing gently until the fruit is soft.

Cut the crusts off the bread and line the
pudding basin. Pour in the fruit and cover
with more slices of bread.

Place a saucer and a weight on top of the
pudding and leave overnight in a cool
place.

Turn out and serve chilled with fresh
cream.

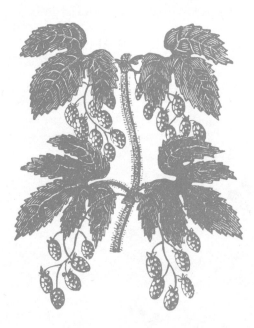

Christmas Plum Pudding

1 pint pudding serves 4

¼ pound plain flour
1 teaspoon salt
1 teaspoon mixed spice
1 teaspoon ground ginger
1 teaspoon ground cinnamon
A pinch of nutmeg, freshly grated
¼ pound fresh white breadcrumbs
½ pound shredded suet
¼ pound soft brown sugar
¼ pound dried apricots, chopped
¼ pound prunes, chopped and stoned
¼ pound dates, chopped and stoned
¼ pound currants
¼ pound sultanas
2 cooking apples, peeled, cored and
   chopped
1 ounce cut mixed peel
2 ounces shredded almonds
Juice and grated rind of an orange
Juice and grated rind of a lemon
¼ pound black treacle
4 large eggs
4 tablespoons brandy

A 3 pint pudding basin, or
three 1 pint pudding basins, well greased
Greaseproof paper, aluminium foil and
string

Sift the flour, salt and spices into a large
mixing bowl and stir in the breadcrumbs,
suet and sugar. Add the chopped dried
fruits, currants, sultanas, apples, peel,
almonds and grated orange and lemon
rind.

Beat the lemon and orange juice, treacle
and eggs together and add to the other
ingredients with the brandy. Mix together
to form a soft consistency.

Turn the mixture into the pudding basin,
cover with greased greaseproof paper and
aluminium foil and secure with string.

Steam for 5 hours for the 3 pint pudding,
or 3½ – 4 hours for the 1 pint puddings.

Steam for at least a further 2 hours
before serving.

Baked Egg Custard

Serves 4 – 6

1 pint milk
3 eggs
1 ounce sugar
Nutmeg, freshly grated

A 1½ pint pie dish, greased
A roasting tin
Foil

Warm the milk in a saucepan, but do not boil.

Whisk the eggs and sugar together in a basin and pour on the hot milk, stirring all the time.

Strain the mixture into the pie dish and sprinkle the top with nutmeg.

Place the dish in a roasting tin surrounded with a little water to slow down the cooking process, so that the custard does not curdle.

Bake at 325°F (Gas Mark 3) for 45 minutes or until set. Allow to cool.

Old English Syllabub

Serves 4

Juice of a large lemon
¼ pint white wine
2 tablespoons brandy
¼ pound caster sugar
½ pint double cream

4 wine glasses
A whisk

Strain the lemon juice into a mixing bowl, add the wine and brandy and sprinkle in the sugar.

Add the double cream to the wine mixture and whisk until it is stiff and holding its shape.

Carefully spoon the syllabub into the wine glasses and chill for at least 1 hour before serving.

Syrup Sponge Pudding

Serves 4 – 6

¼ pound butter
¼ pound caster sugar
2 large eggs, beaten
6 ounces self-raising flour
1 teaspoon ground ginger
2 tablespoons golden syrup
A small quantity of milk

A 1½ pint pudding basin
Greased greaseproof paper
Aluminium foil
String

Cream the butter and sugar together to make them light and fluffy. Gradually add the eggs and beat well until they are thoroughly mixed.

Sift the flour and ground ginger and fold these into the mixture to form a soft consistency – if necessary add a little milk.

Spoon the golden syrup into the base of the pudding basin and put the sponge mixture on top and smooth it over.

Cover with the greased greaseproof paper and foil and secure with string.

Steam for 1½ hours until it has risen well. Serve hot with warmed syrup.

Nottingham Pancake Layer

Serves 6

Batter:
¼ pound plain flour
A pinch of salt
1 egg
Just under ½ pint milk
2 tablespoons water
Filling:
2 pounds Bramley apples, peeled, cored
  and sliced
3 ounces demerara sugar
1 tablespoon lemon juice
1 tablespoon sultanas
2 tablespoons water
Lard for frying
Topping:
1 ounce butter
2 tablespoons granulated sugar

Sift the flour and salt into a mixing bowl, make a well in the centre and break in the egg. Add the milk and water and beat the mixture to make it smooth. Pour in the remaining liquid and beat until it is well mixed.

Place the apples, sugar, lemon juice and sultanas in a pan, cover with the water and cook over a gentle heat to form a thick sauce.

Heat a little lard in a frying pan until it is really hot then pour off any surplus.

Spoon in just enough batter to coat the base of the pan thinly and cook quickly until the pancake is golden brown underneath. Turn with a palette knife and cook the second side. Remove from the pan and keep hot, repeating this process until all the batter is used up.

Place one pancake on an ovenproof dish and spread with the apple sauce. Add another pancake and continue layering, finishing with a pancake.

Melt the butter, pour this over the top of the pancakes and sprinkle with sugar.

Bake at 375°F (Gas Mark 5) for 30 minutes, until the dish is heated through and the sugar has turned to caramel.

Devon Caramel Cream

Serves 6

¼ pound granulated sugar
5 tablespoons water
1 pint milk
4 large eggs
2 ounces caster sugar
A few drops of vanilla essence

1 pint ovenproof mould or tin
A roasting tin

Make the caramel by dissolving the sugar in half the water in a heavy-based pan. Bring to the boil and continue boiling until the caramel is golden brown. Remove from the heat immediately and stir in the remaining cold water. Pour this into the mould or tin and coat the sides with caramel.

Warm the milk in a pan, but do not boil. Whisk the eggs and sugar together in a basin and pour on the warm milk, stirring all the time. Flavour with the vanilla essence, and strain the mixture into the mould.

Place it in the roasting tin and surround it with a little water to slow down the cooking process, so that the custard does not curdle. Cover with foil and bake at 325°F (Gas Mark 3) for 1 hour, or until the custard is firm.

Allow to cool but leave the cream in the mould until it is required then turn out onto a serving dish.

Pickles and Preserves

It is probably in the field of preserving and pickling that the economical mind of the country housewife is most clearly shown. Although it is now so easy to carry stores of food from the abundance of summer into the leaner days of winter, in time gone by it was not so simple and cooks who saw the trees laden with apples and the fields and gardens full of vegetables had to find ways of keeping some of the produce, as well as wanting to make pickles and jellies to accompany the meats they cooked.

Their imaginative use of almost every growing thing as a basis for some kind of preserve meant that they stored away a rare variety of unusual jams and pickles – with so many fresh vegetables and fruits available the mixture of ingredients was endless, all producing delicious flavours.

The recipes in this section are very simple to follow, and they should encourage any housewife who has given her family commercial products in the past because she believed that jam-making and pickling was fraught with enormous difficulties. Some of the ingredients listed in this section are not likely to be growing in your own garden, but once the basic principles of pickling and preserving are understood it will be simple to choose suitable fruit and vegetables when they are plentiful and cheap in the shops. Knowing that a heavy crop of home produce can be preserved will make gardeners less hesitant about growing vegetables;

especially when even the numerous tomatoes that are left green by the vagaries of our weather can be turned into an excellent chutney instead of being discarded.

Quite apart from the extra goodness of these freshly-made preserves, there is great satisfaction to be gained from stocking a corner of your larder with carefully labelled jars of wholesome jams and jellies. From experience most readers will know how popular are the stalls at village fêtes and sales where home-made produce can be bought; and these recipes will enable you to contribute your own preserves to such stalls, or even to make a large batch of jam or pickle at one time so that jars of it can be given as gifts, or exchanged with friends who might have access to completely different ingredients so enabling you to vary the contents of your own cupboard. Although home-made jams and marmalades are always acceptable presents it is possible to produce more exotic preserves at home, and recipes are included for Brandied Peaches and Kentish Pickled Cherries which would both be suitable for Christmas. Mincemeat is popular then, as well, and although it is freely available in the shops it is unlikely you or your family will want to buy it again if once you discover how much better it tastes when it is freshly made.

Spiced Vinegar for Pickling

2 pints malt vinegar
A pinch of mace
A pinch of allspice
A pinch of cloves
¼ inch cinnamon stick
6 peppercorns

Put the vinegar and spices in a pan, bring it to the boil then pour into a bowl.

Cover with a plate and leave for 2 hours. Strain the vinegar and use it as required. *Note:* 2 ounces of pickling spice can be used in place of the 5 ingredients listed above.

Pickled Red Cabbage

1 x 2 pound red cabbage
Salt
2 pints spiced vinegar (see this page)

Cut the cabbage into quarters removing the outer leaves and centre stalks.

Shred the cabbage finely and place a layer of it in a bowl, sprinkled liberally with salt. Make another layer of cabbage and continue these layers until all the cabbage is used. Cover and leave in a cool place overnight.

Drain the cabbage and rinse off any surplus salt. Pack it into jars, pour in the spiced vinegar and cover the jars with lids.

Use within 3 weeks, as the cabbage tends to lose its crispness.

Pickled Walnuts

1 pound green walnuts
1 pint brine, made from 1 pint water
    with 2 ounces salt
2 pints spiced vinegar (see this page)

Cover the walnuts in brine and soak for a week. Change the brine and soak the walnuts for a further week.

Wash and dry well then spread them out on a tray to expose them to the air until they blacken, which takes about a day.

Pack the walnuts into pickle jars and pour in the hot spiced vinegar. Allow to cool and cover with a lid.

Store in a cool place for 6 weeks before use.

Pickled Peaches

4 pounds peaches
1 pint white wine vinegar
¾ pound granulated sugar
A pinch of salt
2 sticks cinnamon
2 teaspoons cloves

Wipe the soft 'down' off the peach skins, prick the fruit all over with a needle and place it in a large bowl.

Boil the vinegar, sugar and salt together in a pan for 15 minutes and pour this over the fruit.

Cover with a plate or aluminium foil and leave to stand for 24 hours.

Strain off the syrup and boil again for 30 minutes. Pour it over the fruit and leave to stand for a further 24 hours.

Place the peaches and syrup in a pan, tie the cinnamon and cloves in a piece of muslin and add this to the pan.

Gently bring to the boil and simmer until the peaches rise to the top of the liquid, then pour the contents back into the bowl to cool.

Remove the muslin bag and pack the pickle into jars, making sure that there is sufficient liquid to cover the fruit completely. Close each pot with a lid and store for 2 weeks before using.

Kentish Pickled Cherries

1 pound granulated sugar
A pinch of allspice
A pinch of mace
A pinch of ground nutmeg
A pinch of cinnamon
2 pounds dark red cherries
½ pint malt vinegar

Mix the sugar and spices together, stone all the cherries and place them in a pan with alternate layers of spiced sugar.

Add the vinegar, bring to the boil and cook for 5 minutes.

Carefully remove the fruit and pack it into jars. Boil the liquor until it thickens and then pour it over the fruit.

Seal with lids and store for 3 months before using.

Brandied Peaches

1 pound fresh firm peaches
½ pound caster sugar
½ pint water
¼ pint brandy

Sugar thermometer

Wash the peaches and plunge them into boiling water for about 10 – 12 seconds to loosen the skins, then put the fruit in cold water so that it is cool enough to handle. Remove the skins carefully, halve the peaches and take out the stones.

Dissolve half the sugar in the water and poach the fruit for 4 – 5 minutes.

Remove from the heat, drain the peaches and allow them to cool. Arrange the fruit in small jars.

Add the remaining sugar to the syrup and dissolve it slowly. Boil to 230°F and allow to cool.

Add the brandy and mix well together. Pour this syrup over the peaches and cover the jars with lids. Store in a cool place, and leave for at least a month before eating.

Lemon Curd

4 ounces butter
Juice and grated rind of 4 large lemons
4 eggs, beaten
1 pound caster sugar

A double saucepan, or a basin standing over a pan of boiling water
2 jam jars and pot covers

Melt the butter in a double saucepan, and add the rind and strained lemon juice.

Stir in the eggs and sugar mixing well until the sugar has dissolved. Continue heating, stirring occasionally, to thicken the lemon curd.

Pour it into the jam jars, seal with pot covers and store in a cool cupboard. The lemon curd should be eaten within a month.

Bitter Orange Marmalade

Makes about 10 pounds

3 pounds Seville oranges
2 lemons
6 pints water
6 pounds preserving or granulated sugar

A preserving pan
A piece of muslin
10 jam jars and pot covers

Wash the oranges and lemons and remove
the peel carefully, making sure that you do
not include any of the white pith. Shred the
peel finely and put it in the preserving pan.

Squeeze the juice from the fruit, save the
pips and tie them up in the muslin. Put this
bag and the juice into the pan with the
peel, add the water and bring to the boil
then simmer gently for about 2 hours until
the peel is really soft and the liquid in the
pan has been reduced by half.

Remove the bag of pips and squeeze it
dry. Stir the sugar into the pan and dissolve it thoroughly, then boil rapidly until
the mixture reaches setting point.

Cool for about 15 minutes, then pour the
marmalade into the jars and seal with pot
covers. Store in a cool place.

Strawberry Jam

Makes about 6 pounds

4 pounds fresh strawberries
4 – 5 tablespoons lemon juice
$3\frac{1}{2}$ pounds preserving or granulated sugar

A preserving pan
5 – 6 jam jars and pot covers

Hull the strawberries and put them into the
preserving pan with the lemon juice.
Simmer the fruit gently in its own juice
for 20 – 30 minutes until it is soft.

Stir in the sugar and dissolve it, boiling
rapidly until setting point is reached. If the
jam is not setting add a little more lemon
juice.

Cool for 15 – 20 minutes, put the jam in
jars, and cover in the usual way.

Grapefruit and Lemon Marmalade

Makes about 5 pounds

large grapefruit
large lemons
pints water
pounds preserving or granulated sugar

A preserving pan
A piece of muslin
jam jars and pot covers

Wash the fruit and remove the peel carefully, making sure that you do not include
any of the white pith. Shred the peel finely
and put it in the preserving pan.

Squeeze the juice from the fruit and put
the pips on one side. Cut the pith off the
squeezed halves of the fruit and put this
with the pips on the muslin and tie them up
together.

Put this bag and the juice in with the
peel, pour the water over it and bring to
the boil, simmering gently for 1½ hours
until the peel is really soft and the contents
of the pan have been reduced by half.

Remove the muslin bag and squeeze it
dry. Stir the sugar into the pan and dissolve
it thoroughly, then boil rapidly until the
mixture reaches setting point.

Cool for about 15 minutes then pour the
marmalade into pots and cover the jars in
the usual way.

Quince and Apple Marmalade

Makes 4 – 5 pounds

2 pounds quince
2 pounds cooking apples
Granulated sugar

A preserving pan
4 – 5 jam jars and pot covers

Pare the quince and apples and place them
in the preserving pan. Cover with water and
simmer until the fruit has formed a pulp.

Press this through a sieve, weigh the
pulp and return it to the pan.

Add the sugar (allowing ¾ pound of sugar
to 1 pound of fruit pulp) and dissolve it,
then simmer gently until the marmalade
reaches setting point.

Cool for 5 – 10 minutes and pour it into
the pots. Cover in the usual way and store
in a cool cupboard.

Mincemeat

1 pound currants
1 pound sultanas
1 pound raisins
½ pound dates, stoned
½ pound cut mixed peel
2 ounces glacé cherries, washed
1 pound cooking apples, grated
½ pound shredded suet
¼ pound almonds, blanched and chopped
1 teaspoon ground nutmeg
1 teaspoon cinnamon
A pinch of mixed spice
Juice and grated rind of 1 lemon
¼ pint brandy or sherry

5 – 6 jam jars and jam covers

Finely chop or mince the dried fruit, peel
and cherries and place them in a large
mixing bowl together with the apples, suet,
almonds and spices. Add the lemon rind
and juice, stirring the mixture thoroughly.

Pour in the brandy, cover and leave to
stand for 2 days in a cool place.

Stir the mincemeat again and pack it into
jars. Cover and store in a cool place. Leave
at least 2 weeks before use.

Dried Apple Rings

4 – 5 pounds apples
2 pints brine, made from 2 pints water and
½ ounce salt

*Several pieces of dowling about 10 inches
long*
An apple corer

Peel and core the apples and cut into rings
about ¼ inch thick. Soak the rings in the
brine for about 10 minutes.

Thread the apple rings on the dowling,
making sure that they do not touch.

Place the apples in the oven, resting the
sticks on the runners of the oven.

Dry in a very cool oven for several hours
until the apples resemble dry chamois
leather but are still moist and pliable.

Cool the apple rings well and store in
airtight containers.

Before using, soak the apple rings in
water for 24 hours.

Apricot Jam

Makes about 6 pounds

1½ pounds apricots
3½ pints water, boiling
Juice of a lemon
3 pounds preserving or granulated sugar
2 ounces almonds, blanched

A preserving pan
5 – 6 jam jars and pot covers

Wash the apricots, drain and place them
in a bowl. Cover with the boiling water and
allow to soak for 24 hours covered with a
plate.

Put the fruit and water into the preserving pan, add the lemon juice, bring to
the boil and simmer for ½ hour, or until the
fruit is soft.

Stir in the sugar until it is dissolved then
add the almonds.

Boil rapidly until setting point is reached,
stirring frequently.

Cool slightly and pour the jam into the
pots. Cover and store in a cool larder.

Green Tomato Chutney

2 pounds green tomatoes, chopped
1 pound cooking apples, peeled, cored and
sliced
½ pound onions, chopped
2 cloves garlic, crushed
¾ pound soft brown sugar
½ pound sultanas
½ pound raisins
1 teaspoon salt
A pinch of cayenne pepper
A pinch of ground ginger
A pinch of cinnamon
A pinch of allspice
¾ pint malt vinegar

Place the tomatoes, apples, onions and
garlic in a preserving pan. Add the sugar,
dried fruit, salt, spices and mix well. Stir
in the vinegar.

Slowly bring to the boil and simmer
gently for about an hour until the chutney
is dark and thick.

Allow the mixture to cool in the pan and
then pour it into pots, cover with tightly
fitting lids and store.

Lemonade in a bottle has now become an accepted part of our lives, and it is hard to believe that not so long ago housewives took for granted that fresh lemons would have to be squeezed before anyone could drink this beverage. To be offered homemade lemonade, in tall glasses clinking with ice on a hot day beneath shady trees captures the real enjoyment of summer in the country. The recipe is so simple you will soon find no excuse for continuing to drink bottled squash.

Ginger beer and barley water are also welcome drinks, and the recipes in this section show that both can be made at home, without any additives. The mysterious workings of yeast enable you to produce vast quantities of Ginger Beer in a corner of even the smallest kitchen. After tasting these cooling drinks it will be easy to understand why farmhouse kitchens used to attract so many visitors.

Many of the traditional country drinks – beef broth, tisanes of herbs, the nutritious Egg Nog and warm possets – were evolved for medicinal purposes, and are still surprisingly comforting in modern times even if they do not possess all the curative powers bestowed on them by legend and hearsay. Mulled Wine, pleasant for the taste of the wine and the warmth of the heat and spices, has long been the drink offered to Carol Singers at Christmas. It is also drunk by the huntsmen at the Meet before they go off for a day's hunting. Therefore such a drink would have ex-

cellent properties for welcoming guests when they arrive in from the cold for a winter party.

No section on country drinks would be complete without a mention of the wide variety of homemade wines, but sadly this book is too small to allow much exploration of this fascinating subject. When farmers' wives first discovered pickling and preserving in sugar and vinegar they also realised the potential of fermentation, and from then on practically everything from cowslip flowers to parsnips were used in homemade wines. These concoctions have enormous potency, and you will be deceived only once by the innocent sound of such drinks as Carrot Whisky.

Finally, no book which has encouraged you to work at such rewarding dishes in the kitchen would be complete without a suggestion for a warm drink at the end of the day that will guarantee a good night's sleep. Throughout the years the soothing properties of malted milk have been acknowledged, and though many commercial products detract from the natural product 'Ovaltine' is the exception because it brings to the consumer in a convenient form all the benefits of the country goodness in barley malt, milk and eggs. So that you can enjoy 'Ovaltine' at its best, we have given detailed instructions on making it.

General Forbes' Ginger Beer

For the ginger beer plant:
2 ounces fresh baker's yeast
2 level tablespoons caster sugar
2 level tablespoons ground ginger
½ pint water

To feed the plant:
10 level teaspoons ground ginger
10 level teaspoons caster sugar

To make the ginger beer:
1 pound 2 ounces caster sugar
1½ pints water
Juice of 2 lemons
6 pints water

Screw-topped bottles (cider bottles are suitable)
A piece of fine muslin

To make the plant, blend the yeast and sugar together until they are smooth. Add the ground ginger and water, transfer the mixture to a jar and cover with a loose-fitting lid.

Each day for 10 days feed the plant with a teaspoon of ground ginger and a teaspoon of caster sugar, stirring well after each addition.

At the end of this time you are ready to make the ginger beer. Dissolve the sugar in the water, bring it to the boil and allow to cool after adding the juice of the lemons.

Pour the ginger mixture through the fine muslin in order to catch the plant, and add the strained liquid to the lemon and sugar syrup.

Add 6 pints of water, stir thoroughly and pour the ginger beer into bottles, sealing them at once.

To make more ginger beer, halve the sediment left on the muslin and place it in separate jars. Add 2 level teaspoons of ground ginger and 2 level teaspoons of caster sugar to each jar and stir well. Continue to feed the plant as before, and make a further batch of beer every 10 days

Egg Nog

Serves 4

2 large eggs
1 tablespoon caster sugar
1 tablespoon brandy
1 pint milk

Beat the egg and sugar together until thick and creamy then stir in the brandy.

Bring the milk to the boil and pour it on the egg mixture, whisking well. Pour into glasses and serve at once.

Posset

Serves 1 – 2

2 thin slices stale bread
A pinch of salt
A pinch of nutmeg, freshly grated
1 tablespoon caster sugar
1 pint milk
2 tablespoons sherry

Cut the bread into small dice, and put these in a soup bowl.

Sprinkle on the salt, grated nutmeg and sugar.

Bring the milk to the boil and pour this over the bread. Allow to stand, covered, for 10 minutes then stir in the sherry and serve.

Honeysuckle Cup

Makes about 2½ pints

bottle dry white wine
tablespoons honey
small glass Cointreau
wine glass brandy
½ pints fizzy lemonade
lemon, sliced
orange, sliced
peach, stoned and sliced
Crushed ice

Mix the wine, honey, Cointreau, brandy
and lemonade together.

Place the sliced fruit and ice in a bowl
and pour the wine mixture over them.

Allow to stand for 1 hour before serving.

Lemon and Orange Squash

Makes about 1¼ pints

2 pounds granulated sugar
1½ pints water
Juice and grated rind of 3 large lemons
Juice and grated rind of 2 large oranges
4 level teaspoons tartaric acid

Dissolve the sugar and water in a pan,
bring to the boil and simmer for about 10
minutes.

Place the lemon and orange rind in a
bowl with the tartaric acid and pour in the
sugar syrup, mixing well.

Cover and leave to stand for 24 hours,
then strain in the lemon and orange juice.

Pour the squash into bottles and seal.
Store in a cool place, and dilute to taste
with water.

Mulled Wine

Makes 1½ pints

Juice of 2 large oranges
Juice of 2 large lemons
4 cloves
2 inch stick cinnamon
1 level teaspoon ground nutmeg
¼ pound sugar
1 bottle dry red wine
¼ pint brandy
1 orange, sliced
1 apple, cored and sliced

Strain the orange and lemon juice into a pan, add the cloves and spices and stir in the sugar.

Dissolve it gently then bring the juice to the boil. Allow it to cool and add the wine. Heat the mixture but do not let it boil, then pour in the brandy.

Strain the wine into a bowl and stir in the orange and apple slices.

An Excellent Cup of Ovaltine

Serves: 1

A cup of milk
2 teaspoons of Ovaltine
Sugar to taste

Heat the milk until it is almost boiling, then pour it into the cup. Stir in two or more heaped teaspoons of Ovaltine. Some people may like to add extra sugar although most find it already sweet enough.

Refreshing Grapefruit Barley Water

Makes 2 pints

4 ounces pearl barley
2 pints water
4 ounces sugar
2 large grapefruit
1 lemon

Put the pearl barley into a pan, with just enough water to cover it, and bring to the boil. Strain off the liquid and rinse the barley under cold running water.

Return the barley to the pan, pour in the 2 pints of water, bring to the boil again then cover and simmer for about 1 hour.

Strain the liquid into a jug, adding the sugar and stirring well before allowing the mixture to cool.

Extract the juice from the grapefruit and lemon and strain this into the barley liquor. Store in a screw topped jar in the refrigerator.

Traditional 18th century Spiced Ale

1 quart brown ale
Grated rind of half lemon
1 teaspoon ground ginger
1 teaspoon ground nutmeg
1 stick cinnamon
3 eggs
3 ounces soft brown sugar
¼ pint brandy
¼ pint rum

Heat the ale, lemon rind and spices together in a large saucepan. Meanwhile make a poker red hot and plunge it into the ale, holding it there until the bubbling subsides.

Whip the sugar and eggs together until frothy. Warm the brandy and rum together in a small pan, pour this into the ale mixture, and combine. Whisk well until smooth and creamy, and serve at once.

Savouries and Snacks

Nowadays the conventional ending to a meal is a sweet course, though at one time a savoury such as Devils on Horseback or Scotch Woodcock was very popular as the final course. Today the need for a savoury taste at the end of a meal is generally satisfied by cheese, and the savouries have been adopted as snacks and light supper dishes. Welsh Rarebit or Devilled Chicken Livers make strongly flavoured and satisfying quick meals, whilst Yorkshire Bacon Custards and Potted Cheese are suitable for the first course of a dinner party menu.

Unfortunately we are limited by space from enlarging this section to include all the other snacks and savouries that taste so good when made with fresh country produce – omelettes, with various fillings, scrambled eggs with herbs, cheese cooked in all kinds of ways (some mentioned in the Cheese section further on in the book) – even a boiled egg is a delicacy when it is really fresh. Bacon, which tends to taste always the same when vacuum-packed, does have a magnificent flavour when you buy it freshly sliced. If so, bacon and eggs can become a really fine feast.

In the country it is still possible to find a butcher who produces his own brawn, freshly made from pork trimmings and set solid in its own juices. A few slices of this with homemade preserve, a green salad and a glass of milk will make a more nourishing snack than the usual 'cup of tea and a sandwich'. This same butcher might also make his own sausages, using just minced lean pork meat and a flavouring of herbs. Even the heartiest of appetites will be satisfied by several plump sausages, grilled, with a few field mushrooms and sautéed potatoes. Mushrooms grow wild in parts of the countryside, and are well worth hunting for on warm misty mornings just to discover the taste that has never been captured by the white varieties that grow in total darkness. Maybe some of these things seem very remote to the housewife who does her weekly shopping in a large supermarket, but sometime she will leave the town, perhaps for a holiday, and it will be part of her pleasure to know these delights still exist in the country.

Fried Cod's Roe

Serves 4

¾ pound hard cod's roe, cooked
1 egg, beaten
¼ pound fresh white breadcrumbs
Oil for frying
Lemon wedges

A deep frying pan
Absorbent kitchen paper

Cut the cod's roe into thick slices and coat
each piece in beaten egg and breadcrumbs.

Heat the oil in a pan and fry the roe
in the fat until it is crisp and golden brown.

Drain well on absorbent kitchen paper
and place on a hot serving dish.

Garnish with lemon wedges and serve at
once.

Bloater Toasts

Serves 4

2 bloaters
A small quantity of oil
1 ounce butter, softened
1 tablespoon parsley, chopped
Cayenne pepper
1 teaspoon lemon juice
4 slices bread

A mortar and pestle or electric liquidiser

Soak the bloaters in boiling water for 2 – 3
minutes and drain well. Remove the heads
and fins, roes and backbone then clean the
flesh.

Place on a grill grid, brush over with a
little oil and cook for about 5 minutes on
each side until the fish is cooked thoroughly. Allow to cool, then pound down in a
mortar and pestle or blend in a liquidiser
until the fish is creamy.

Blend the bloaters, butter, parsley,
cayenne pepper and lemon juice together.

Toast the bread on both sides and spread
the bloater paste on each slice. Return
them under the grill until they are heated
through, cut into fingers and serve at once.

Scotch Woodcock

Serves 4

4 slices bread
Anchovy paste or Gentleman's Relish
1 ounce butter
4 tablespoons cream
2 eggs, beaten
A pinch of cayenne pepper

Toast the bread on both sides, remove the
crusts and spread with the anchovy paste.

Gently melt the butter in a pan. Mix the
cream, eggs and cayenne pepper together
and season with salt and pepper.

Add the egg mixture to the pan and cook
until it begins to thicken.

Remove the pan from the heat and stir
until the mixture is creamy then spread it
over the anchovy toast and serve at once.

Devils on Horseback

Serves 4

1 tablespoon oil
4 whole almonds, blanched
4 large prunes, soaked until plump
2 rashers streaky bacon
1 ounce butter
4 rounds bread about 2 inches in diameter
Watercress

4 Cocktail sticks
Absorbent kitchen paper

Melt the oil in a pan and fry the almonds
gently until they are golden brown.

Drain the prunes and dry well, carefully
removing each stone and putting an almond
in its place.

Cut the bacon in half, wrap it round each
prune and secure with a cocktail stick.

Place the Devils on Horseback under a
hot grill and cook until they are golden
brown.

Meanwhile, melt the butter in a pan and
fry the bread rounds until they are crisp.
Drain well on absorbent paper.

Place on a hot serving dish and top with
the prunes. Garnish with watercress and
serve very hot.

Welsh Rarebit

Serves 4 – 6

½ pound Cheddar cheese, grated
1 ounce butter
1 teaspoon dry mustard
A few drops of Worcestershire sauce
4 tablespoons brown ale
1 tablespoon parsley, chopped
4 – 6 thick slices of bread

Place the cheese and butter in a heavy-based pan and melt carefully. Add the mustard, Worcestershire sauce and brown ale.

Stir well and mix in the fresh parsley, seasoning with salt and pepper.

Toast the bread on both sides and spread with the rarebit mixture. Place under the grill until the cheese is golden brown and bubbling. Serve hot.

Yorkshire Bacon Custards

¼ pound shortcrust pastry
2 rashers back bacon, chopped
2 eggs, beaten
2 tablespoons cream
Parsley

Small patty tins
1½ inch cutter

Roll out the pastry on a floured pastry board and cut into rounds with the pastry cutter.

Line the patty tins with the pastry rounds, and divide the bacon pieces between the tins.

Beat the eggs and cream together and season well with salt and pepper.

Pour a little of the egg mixture into each pastry case and bake at 400°F (Gas Mark 6) for 15 minutes or until golden brown.

Serve hot or cold garnished with parsley sprigs.

Devilled Chicken Livers

Serves 4

4 chicken livers
1 ounce butter
1 shallot, finely chopped
1 teaspoon parsley, chopped
Cayenne pepper
2 rashers streaky bacon
1 ounce butter
4 rounds of bread 2 inches in diameter

8 cocktail sticks

Wash and dry the chicken livers and cut each one in half. Melt a little butter in a pan and fry the shallot until it is transparent. Mix in the parsley and cayenne pepper and season with salt.

Cut each rasher into four pieces, wrap them round each piece of chicken liver and secure with a cocktail stick. Place the chicken livers and shallot mixture in an ovenproof dish, cover and bake at 400°F (Gas Mark 6) for 15 – 20 minutes.

Meanwhile, melt the butter in a pan and fry the bread rounds until they are golden brown. Place on a hot serving dish with the devilled chicken livers on top. Serve hot.

Potted Cheese

2 ounces Cheddar cheese
2 ounces Cheshire cheese
2 ounces Stilton
3 ounces butter, softened
Parsley, chopped
Chives, chopped
3 tablespoons port

Grate the cheeses finely and mix together in a bowl. Add the butter and beat the ingredients together thoroughly.

Add the chopped parsley and chives and pour in the port, mixing well.

Press into small dishes and smooth the top. Cover with a lid or aluminium foil and store in a cool place.

Serve with hot buttered toast.

Cheeses

The first English cheese factory was set up in Derby in 1870, and since then the large scale manufacture of cheese has become more and more sophisticated. By the early 1960s, cheese manufacture had been almost completely mechanised. The improved techniques have produced cheeses with a consistent high quality and uniformity of taste and texture. Cheese now matures in an environment of carefully controlled temperature and humidity, with grading and sorting taking place before the cheese is packaged and distributed to the shops and supermarkets. However, farms throughout the country still produce their own farmhouse cheeses, which are in short supply and have an excellent reputation.

It takes one gallon of milk to make one pound of cheese. The milk is first clotted by either allowing it to sour or by adding rennet. When the curd has formed it is cut into pieces, salted, heated, stirred and drained. The curd is then moulded in a cloth-lined mould of a traditional size and shape, according to the type of cheese required. The curd is pressed if a hard cheese is required, but for a soft cheese which has an open texture, pressure is not applied. Cheeses such as Stilton are injected with stainless steel needles containing penicillium mould at the curd stage, and the cheese is allowed to ripen. The ripening stage ranges from ten days to six months.

Cottage cheese is made of cooked skimmed milk curd, which is drained, washed in cold water, and then given a very thin coating of cream. Cottage cheese contains only 4% fat. Curd cheese is made from whole milk and contains 12% fat, while in cream cheese the fat content is as much as 50%.

Regional preferences can play a large part in the colouring of cheese. Cheshire cheese is preferred white in the region of its origin, whilst the rest of the country has come to expect Cheshire to be a red cheese. Other cheeses are popular in different regions; Red Cheddar, which is generally made in New Zealand, is popular in East Anglia and Scotland. Caerphilly has been for generations the miners cheese because it is digestible, even when eaten in large quantities, moist in texture and mild, but salty in flavour, which makes it ideal for the hot, thirsty conditions below ground.

Caerphilly was originally a Welsh cheese, but it is now made in the West Country. It is an economical cheese to make as it matures within 3 weeks.

Cheddar is probably the best known and most widely used of English cheeses. It was originally made in Cheddar in Somerset, but due to its popularity, it is also produced in large quantities in other parts of the country and in Ireland, Canada, Australia and New Zealand where a special process of 'cheddarizing' is widely used. Pasteurized milk is poured into a vast steam-jacketed vat, to which a 'starter' of milk-souring bacteria is added and then rennet is introduced to coagulate the milk. Up to this point the process is similar to other cheeses, but now the 'cheddarizing' beings). When the curd has hardened to a moderate firmness, it is cut into half inch cubes. As the whey separates, the curd is gently heated to about 100°F and stirred for about one hour. The pieces of curd shrink and harden under the increasing acidity of the whey and finally settle into a solid mass at the bottom of the vat. This mass, cut into blocks, turned at intervals and cut into strips, is piled into high stacks, so that its own weight helps to press out the whey. The curd is put through a mill and broken into small pieces which are salted and cooled. It is then placed into cloth-lined cylindrical moulds 12 inches in diameter and 11 inches high and pressed before ripening, which takes between three and six months.

Farmhouse cheddar is made with whole unpasteurized summer milk taken from a single herd of cows. The process is basically the same as for factory-made cheese, but the batches are smaller and they are matured for a longer time

Cheshire is believed to be several hundred years older than Cheddar cheese. The red cheese, which is milder in flavour than the white, used to be coloured with marigold or carrot juice, but now it is artificially coloured. Occasionally a red Cheshire cheese will develop blue veins, giving the cheese a fine rich texture and flavour.

Derby is at its peak when it is six months old and after this its flavour and texture deteriorate. Sage Derby is made by adding chopped fresh sage leaves to the curds before pressing, which gives the cheese a green marbled appearance.

Double Gloucester is tinted with annotto dye for the London market, but locally it is left in its natural creamy colour. Single Gloucester is the same shape as the double one, but is only half as thick, and can be eaten earlier during the ripening process – at about six weeks. The cheese does not travel well and is seldom seen outside its own area.

Lancashire has been known throughout its history as 'old toaster' because it is an excellent cheese for cooking, melting into a rich creamy sauce. It used to be the staple food of the Lancashire mill workers in the cotton towns and it is still sometimes crumbled over Lancashire hot pot to give it extra flavour.

Leicester was originally dyed flame red colour with marigold and carrot juice as a sales gimmick, but it was not intended to alter the flavour. The cheese still maintains its brilliant colour, which is achieved by the addition of annotto dye.

Genuine Stilton, made in Stilton in Huntingdonshire, Leicestershire and Rutland is the king of British cheeses. Farmhouse Stiltons used to take eighteen months to mature. Now, the process need only take four months, although the cheese benefits from longer maturing. It takes seventeen gallons of milk to make a 14 pound Stilton. It should be cut across its width and not spooned out of the crust. Contrary to belief it is unforgivable to drench a good Stilton with port – this should be drunk separately! White Stilton is a pleasant undistinguished cheese, and bears little resemblance to the blue veined variety.

White Wensleydale comes from the Ure valley in Yorkshire, where it was first made by monks. The original cheese was marbled and had a creamy Cheddar-like taste with a hint of honey. Blue Wensleydale, which resembles Stilton in shape and flavour (although it is milder), requires considerable time and care in its preparation, hence it is becoming more and more scarce.

Cheese is one of the most nutritious of foods, containing approximately 30%

protein, 30% fat, and 30% water, and yielding an average of 120 calories per ounce. It contains as much protein per ounce as three ounces of lean meat.

Cheese should be stored in a cool place, preferably not a refrigerator, as this tends to dry the cheese and deaden the taste. Wrap it loosely in waxed or greaseproof paper. If mould should form on the surface cut it away and use the cheese as soon as possible.

Hard cheese is best for grating and may be mixed with breadcrumbs as a topping for grilled or baked savoury dishes or it may be used in sauces to serve with vegetables or fish.

Type of cheese	Description	Uses
Caerphilly	A whole-milk close-textured cheese with a mild and slightly salty flavour	Ideal to eat in salads, or with fruit and apple pie, but not a good cooking cheese
Cheddar	A hard cheese with a close texture. Its flavour is clean, mellow and nutty, varying from mild to strong depending on age	Suitable for eating cooked or uncooked. An excellent grating and cooking cheese delicious with gingerbread and fruit pies
Cheshire	A savoury, crumbly-textured faintly salty hard cheese, white and red with blue veins	Equally good cooked or uncooked. Recommended for toasting and Welsh rarebits
Derby	A hard close-textured pressed white cheese with a clean and tangy flavour. Sage Derby is mottled with green	Derby is not a cooking cheese, but it is excellent for a cheeseboard and delicious with fresh fruit
Double Gloucester	An orange-yellow hard cheese with a buttery, open texture. It has a creamy and delicate flavour	A cheese which is equally good cooked or uncooked. Use in flans and sauces
Lancashire	A white cheese with a soft crumbly texture and a clean mild flavour	Considered to be the best cooking cheese available, melting into a rich creamy sauce
Leicester	A hard orange cheese with a crumbly and open texture. Its flavour is mild and mellow	Excellent for use in cooked dishes and delicious with celery and fresh fruit
Stilton	A white semi-hard cheese with blue veining. Stilton has a soft close texture and a rich creamy flavour, with considerable body	An 'after dinner' cheese, which should be included on every cheeseboard
Wensleydale	A soft and close-textured firm cheese, either white or blue with a clean lingering flavour	The delicate taste makes Wensleydale unsuitable for cooking, but it is a good cheese for spreading

This glossary is intended to help readers with any technical words in recipes from the book; but it is hoped that any unusual cookery terms encountered elsewhere will also be explained here so that this book continues in use even after all the recipes have become familiar.

Aerating To mix air into flour by passing it through a sieve or letting it fall through the fingers.

Bake To cook by means of dry heat in the oven.

Baste To spoon hot fat or stock over food as it roasts in order to keep the food succulent and moist.

Batter A mixture of egg, flour and milk, beaten together to form a smooth liquid. Used to make pancakes and puddings.

Blanch To whiten meat, vegetables and rice. The food is covered with cold water and brought to the boil, then strained off. This method is also used to remove the skins from almonds.

Blind To cook pastry, for tarts or flans, without a filling. Line the flan ring with pastry and cover with a circle of grease-proof paper, or aluminium foil. Half-fill with baking beans or stale crusts of bread. Bake, either completely or partially, as directed in the recipe.

Boil To cook in water at 212°F. As the liquid reaches this temperature it will bubble indicating that boiling point has been reached.

Braise To cook slowly by a moist heat. It is a combination of stewing, steaming and pot roasting. The meat or vegetables are browned quickly and placed in a covered pan with a small amount of liquid and cooked slowly.

Bran The inner husk of grain which is separated by grinding. Bran is removed from white flour, but it remains in whole-meal flour.

Brawn Generally made from a pig's head, (but oxtail and other meats may be used) which is stewed until the meat can be picked off the bones, and the remaining liquid poured over it which sets to produce a jelly. The brawn is sliced and eaten cold.

Bunch of herbs *or bouquet garni* A combination of herbs contained in a small muslin bag, usually consisting of a bayleaf, a few sprigs of thyme, parsley, peppercorns and marjoram. Fresh herbs should be used whenever possible, and the bag removed from the dish before it is served.

Caramel A syrup made from 1 pound of sugar to 1 pint water, boiled until it turns golden brown. Used for flavouring sweet sauces and custards, and sometimes for decoration.

Clarify To clear or purify. Boiling water is added to melted dripping and allowed to cool. The clean fat floats to the top and when solidified it can be lifted off. To clarify butter or margarine, the fat is melted without browning and then cooled to allow the sediment to drop to the bottom – if necessary the fat should be poured through muslin. Egg whites are used to clarify meat, broths and jellies. The egg white is whisked into the mixture and brought to the boil, which causes it to rise to the top of the mixture carrying with it any opaque matter. The liquid should be poured through a jelly bag, resulting in crystal clear jelly or stock.

Coating To cover food with flour, egg and breadcrumbs or batter when it is to be fried or grilled. Also to cover food with a sauce, salad cream or fresh cream.

Compote Fruit which has been poached in a syrup made from sugar and water.

Condiments Spices and seasonings such as salt, pepper and mustard which add flavour and piquancy to a dish.

Cream To beat together fat and sugar until it is pale and fluffy. and resembles whipped cream in colour and texture. This method is used for cakes, fillings and biscuits.

Curd The solid part of sour milk or junket, or the creamy preserve made from eggs, butter. lemon and oranges.

Curing A method of preserving meat and fish by subjecting to salt, sugar and salt-petre. The methods involve dry salting and pickling in brine. The major ingredient is salt and sugar is used to counteract the hardening effect of the saltpetre which is used to give the meat colour.

Devilled To make food peppery, spiced and hot in taste.

Dredge To sprinkle flour and sugar lightly using a perforated dredger.

Dripping The fat obtained from roasted meat, beef being the best for most purposes. Dripping can be used for frying, roasting and shortening cakes, bread and pastry. The gravy sediments can be added to soups and stocks.

Duchesse Potato which has been boiled and puréed with butter, cream and egg yolk, and then piped into the shape required. The potato is brushed with beaten egg and browned in the oven or under the grill.

Faggot or Fagot Minced meat (often liver) lightly seasoned and baked, and usually reheated before eating. Also a bunch of herbs.

Farce, forcemeat Stuffing used for meat, fish or vegetables. The basic ingredients are generally breadcrumbs, onions, suet, herbs and eggs.

Fines Herbes A mixture of chopped herbs such as parsley, thyme, chervil, marjoram, for making herb butter, omelettes or for adding to forcemeats.

Flake To separate the flesh of cooked fish into flakes using a fork.

Flan A shallow pastry case, usually baked blind containing sweet or savoury fillings.

Folding-in To combine a whisked or cream mixture with other ingredients so that it retains its lightness. This method is used for cakes. meringues and desserts.

Fool A mixture which is made up with two parts of fruit purée and one part of fresh cream, and served chilled.

Frying To cook in hot fat. There are two kinds of frying – shallow frying in a wide, open pan, and deep frying in a large, deep saucepan or chip pan. Shallow frying may also be termed 'dry frying' when the only fat used is that which runs from the food being cooked, as with bacon and sausages. A thin coating of fat is required for cooking pancakes and eggs, and about a half-inch depth is required for meat balls, potatoes, fish and fishcakes. When deep frying, the pan should be only one-third filled with oil, and the temperature of the oil may be either 350°F for raw foods or 375°F for cooked foods and chips. If a frying thermometer is not available the temperature can be gauged by dropping a small cube of bread into the fat. If it rises to the top and becomes golden brown in 55 seconds the temperature is about 350°F, and if the bread browns in 45 seconds the temperature is about 375°F.

Garnish An edible decoration, such as parsley, hard-boiled egg, watercress or lemon, used to make a savoury dish more attractive.

Girdle Known also as Griddle. An iron plate about $\frac{1}{4}$ inch thick, used for baking cakes and scones.

Glaze To add a gloss to the surface of a dish by coating with a sweet or savoury sauce, or brushing with beaten egg, milk or sugar syrup.

Infuse To soak or steep vegetables, herbs and spices in a warm or cold liquid to extract the flavour – generally used for savoury sauces.

Knead To work together into a smooth dough. Gentle kneading is required for pastry, scone and biscuit mixtures, whereas firmer and prolonged kneading with the 'heel' of the hand is required for bread.

Larding To thread strips of fat bacon, using a 'larding' needle, into the surface of lean meat before roasting, grilling and braising to prevent it drying out during cooking.

Marinade Originally the brine used to pickle fish before cooking, now used to flavour and tenderise the food. The marinade usually consists of oil, wine, sliced onions, herbs and spices.

Meringue A mixture made from stiffly beaten egg whites and caster sugar which is dried until crisp in a slow oven.

Mortar and Pestle The mortar, or bowl, is generally made of metal, marble, stone or wood, and the pestle is made of wood. A mortar and pestle is used for pounding meat and fish and for mixing and crushing herbs and spices.

Mould A metal or china receptacle to hold a mixture in a certain shape while it sets, or is baked. A mould is generally used for ices, desserts, jellies, puddings, bread or rice rings, and pressed meat.

Mousse A smooth textured sweet or savoury cream, generally based on eggs and cream and sometimes using gelatine to set the dish.

Offal The edible internal parts of an animal, of which the most usual are liver, kidney, heart, tongue, tripe, sweetbreads, brains, melts and lights.

Parboil To partly cook before completing the cooking by another process.

Pare To peel or trim, generally used in connection with vegetables and fruit.

Pastry Cream A traditional filling for patisseries. Made by boiling flour, cornflour, egg yolks, milk and sugar together and then folding in egg whites. Flavoured by vanilla, almond essence, chocolate or coffee and used in flans, tarts and gateaux.

Pectin A natural gum-like substance which is present in most ripe fruits and is essential to obtain a good set in jams and jellies.

Poaching To cook eggs, fish and some meat dishes in an uncovered pan at simmering point with sufficient liquid to cover.

Praline A mixture of burnt sugar and almonds which is crushed and added to creams, ices and soufflés.

Purée A smooth pulp or cream of vegetables or fruit which has been passed through a sieve or blended in a liquidiser.

Raspings Dried, sieved breadcrumbs used for egg and crumb coating. To make raspings, put stale bread to dry in a slow oven, cool it, then sieve and store in an airtight tin.

Reduce To thicken or concentrate the flavour of a sauce or gravy by boiling away some of the water content.

Render To extract the fat from meat trimmings by warming them in an oven until the fat has melted, or by boiling the meat fat and a little water in an uncovered pan until the water has evaporated and the fat has melted. It is then strained through muslin.

Rennet It is obtained from the stomach of a calf, and is used for making junket by coagulating milk. It is also used for making cheese.

Roux A mixture made with melted butter and flour which is cooked and used as the basis of white and brown sauces.

Saltpetre Nitrate of potash used in the process of pickling meats and fish.

Sauces There are two main kinds – a 'coating' sauce which must be thick enough when it reaches boiling point to coat the back of a wooden spoon, and a 'pouring' sauce which, when it reaches boiling point, must only glaze the back of a spoon.

Sauté To toss or shake the food in fat until it is golden brown.

Scald To plunge into boiling water for easy peeling or to bring a liquid just to the boil.

Score To slash, with a sharp knife, just through the surface of the food.

Seasoned flour Used for dusting meat and fish before frying or stewing. It is made by adding salt and pepper, and sometimes herbs, to flour which adds flavour to the food.

Setting point A term used to indicate that jam or marmalade is ready for bottling. A sugar thermometer is the most accurate method of telling when setting point has been reached. When the temperature reaches 221°F the jam is ready. If you do not have a sugar thermometer or you wish to double check setting point, remove the pan from the heat and put a very small amount of jam on a cold saucer. Allow it to cool, draw your finger across the top of the jam and if the surface wrinkles, setting point has been reached. If the jam is not ready continue boiling it for a few minutes and test again.

Shortening A lard or vegetable fat which contains no liquid and hence gives a very 'short' or crisp texture when rubbed into flour for baking.

Sieve To rub cooked food through a sieve, using a wooden spoon to press it down.

Sift To shake dry ingredients through a sieve or flour sifter to remove lumps and to aerate the dry ingredients.

Simmer To keep a liquid just below boiling point. The surface of the liquid should be just moving but not bubbling.

Skim To remove fat off the surface of stock, gravies, sauces and stews, or the scum from jams and jellies.

Soufflé An egg dish which is either sweet or savoury, hot or cold. A soufflé is a very light mixture and raised only by the stiffly whisked egg whites. Hot soufflés are usually made with cheese and vegetable purées, bound with a thick white sauce before beating in the egg yolks and folding in the egg whites and then baked in a special ovenproof dish. Cold soufflés have cream and eggs, and are set with gelatine.

Soured Cream This is cream that has been artificially soured before sale. Cream can be soured at home by the addition of lemon juice or vinegar.

Steaming To cook food in the steam from boiling water. A special steamer which fits on top of a saucepan can be used, or the food can be placed in a covered mould or bowl in a pan with the water halfway up the sides of the bowl and covered with a tightly fitting lid. This method of cooking is used for fish, meat, puddings and vegetables.

Steep To pour hot or cold water over food and then leave it to stand, either to soften it or to extract the flavour and colour.

Stock A liquid made by simmering bones, scraps of meat or fish, sometimes with the addition of vegetables, to extract the flavour. Stock is the basis of soups, sauces and stews.

Strong flour A special flour suitable for breadmaking because it has properties that produce an elastic dough which rises well. It is widely available from grocers and healthfood stores.

Thickening To give body to soups, sauces and gravies by the addition of flour, cornflour, arrowroot, egg yolks, butter or cream.

Truss To tie or skewer a bird into a compact shape before roasting.

Waterbath or *bain-marie* A shallow container filled with hot water in which to cook a sauce, pudding or custard to prevent the dish overheating and therefore curdling during cooking.

Whip or Whisk To beat air rapidly into a mixture using a fork or a rotary electric beater.

Zest The oil which gives the flavour to orange and lemon peel and which can be removed by grating or rubbing it with a lump of sugar.

Weights and Measures

Dry Ingredients		Approximate metric measurement used to simplify conversion (in grammes)	Liquid Ingredients		Approximate metric measurement used to simplify conversion (in millilitres)
Imperial measurement (in ounces)	Exact metric conversion (in grammes)		Imperial measurement (in fluid ounces)	Exact metric conversion (in millilitres)	
1	28.35	25	1	28.35	25
2	56.70	50	2	56.70	50
4	113.40	100	5	141.75	125
8	226.80	200	10	283.50	250
12	340.20	300	15	452.25	375
16	453.60	400	20	567.00	500
32	907.20	1 kilogram	35	992.25	1 litre

When using 25 as the basic metric unit in a recipe, the end result will yield slightly less than the original by about 2 ounces (50 grammes) to 1 pound of flour.

Oven temperatures

Electric scale °Fahrenheit	Electric scale °Centigrade	Gas oven marks
225°F	110°C	$\frac{1}{4}$
250°F	130°C	$\frac{1}{2}$
275°F	140°C	1
300°F	150°C	2
325°F	170°C	3
350°F	180°C	4
375°F	190°C	5
400°F	200°C	6
425°F	220°C	7
450°F	230°C	8
475°F	240°C	9

Index

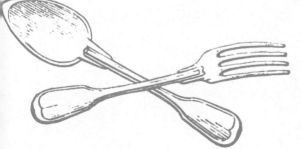

Pickles and Preserves

78 Apple Rings, dried
78 Apricot Jam
75 Cherries, pickled
78 Green Tomato Chutney
75 Lemon Curd
76 Marmalade, Bitter Orange
77 Marmalade, Grapefruit and Lemon
77 Marmalade, Quince and Apple
77 Mincemeat
75 Peaches, brandied
74 Peaches, pickled
74 Red Cabbage, pickled
76 Strawberry Jam
74 Vinegar, spiced for pickling
74 Walnuts, pickled

Drinks

80 Egg Nog
80 Ginger Beer
82 Grapefruit Barley Water
81 Honeysuckle Cup
81 Lemon Squash
82 Mulled Wine
81 Orange Squash
82 Ovaltine
80 Posset
82 Spiced Ale

Savouries and Snacks

84 Bloater Toasts
84 Cod's Roe, fried
85 Devilled Chicken Livers
84 Devils on Horseback
85 Potted Cheese
84 Scotch Woodcock
85 Welsh Rarebit
85 Yorkshire Bacon Custards